THE SACRED GIFT OF FIRE

An intense collection of erotic poetry and prose.

From the heart, soul, and mind of:
Clyde R. Hurlston

copyright © 2022 by Clyde Hurlston. All rights reserved. Printed in the United States Of America. This book may not be reproduced or reprinted, unless in the context of reviews, without prior approval from the author unless otherwise stated.

On behalf of the author, thank you for your purchase.
And may The Hermetic Principles guide us all.

www.clydehurlston.com
facebook.com/adebtpaidinink
@adebtpaidinink

THE SACRED GIFT OF FIRE

CLYDE HURLSTON

"Man is the animal who weeps and laughs - and writes. If the first Prometheus brought fire from Heaven in a fennel-stalk, the last will take it back - in a book."

- *John Cowper Powys*

"Playing God is indeed playing with fire. But that is what we mortals have done since Prometheus, the patron saint of dangerous discoveries. We play with fire and take the consequences, because the alternative is cowardice in the face of the unknown."

- *Ronald Dworkin*

"Why should the thirst for knowledge be aroused, only to be disappointed and punished? My volition shrinks from the painful task of recalling my humiliation; yet, like a second Prometheus, I will endure this and worse, if by any means I may arouse in the interiors of Plane and Solid Humanity a spirit of rebellion against the Conceit which would limit our Dimensions to Two or Three or any number short of infinity."

- *Edwin Abbott Abbott*

ACT I
The Alchemy Of Desire

"To burn with desire and keep quiet about it,
is the greatest punishment we can bring on ourselves."
- Federico Garcia Lorca

"Desire is in men a hunger, in women only an appetite."
- Mignon McLaughlin

CLYDE HURLSTON

"Conjuring The Goddess" Art by Sir Render

SECRETS BLOOM IN GRAVES

Tell me something, darling...
And it will stay just between us.
What is the thing that your body craves?
What is the thought that never leaves you alone,
And always keeps you warm
Down in the most sacred of places?
Will you share it with me?
Can you take advantage
of my knack for keeping secrets?
Knowing that I will take so many things to the grave.
Do you need to make that confession, baby?
Feel free to do so.
For you are always safe with me.
Whether you want to instruct or be punished,
I'm ready to grant your wish.
I just need to know if you're brave enough
To pay the purest pleasure's price.
See? I'm not asking for forever, baby.
With what I have in mind,
A few hours will suffice.

CLYDE HURLSTON

RAVENOUS

They don't know what it's like.
They don't see me pacing in the darkness.
They're too busy being content.
They don't know what it's like to see such
magnificence, and to be overlooked by it.
They have never felt the ache within their bones.
Waiting for a lover that will never come.
To be foaming at the mouth with impatience,
is to be starved until ravenous.
And for her, I am all of the above.
I curse her name a thousand times,
for it is more than my anger that rises.
And she isn't here to alleviate this pain.
My medicine walks upright
and she is too far for me to reach.
I'm going crazy in this cage.
And imagination no longer holds the key.
Only the real thing will suffice,
or else this world must be forced
to pay the eternal price.

SLEEPING GIANTS

My heart and soul were sleeping giants
And you just couldn't let them lie.
Now they're stomping through the village.
And you've the nerve to ask me why.
After several decades worth of slumber
Something finally made them stir.
And now you're playing coy
As if you didn't cause this to occur.
But who else could put me in a state,
Where I'd turn into a fiend?
That wants to overdose inside,
The one who makes my reality a dream.
For your look can give me chills,
A kiss can cause my pulse to race.
My heart calls out for war
When you're beside me in this space.
So won't you come and calm the giants,
With your intoxicating ways?
And do something about,
This monolith you've raised.

CLYDE HURLSTON

DEATH SENTENCE

Here I am again.
In that all too familiar place.
Burning with desire,
hiding ashes that smell of desperation.
But in reality, I shouldn't.
For pride is of no use to the kneeling.
Fuck the world and their petty judgments.
Let them know the truth: I ache for you.
I beg for you in my very dreams.
The waves of my lust
cause more than the tides to rise,
at the merest mention of your name.
I climb the lonely walls of this bell tower,
hoping you'll return again.
The hands of that goddamn clock,
they bring out the masochist in me.
They might as well be around my neck,
since I don't want to breathe until you're near.
Come back, baby.
For the love of everything holy,
take me back to Heaven with a look.
Make my heart call out for war,
as if it were born in ancient Sparta.
And use your touch, baby.
Help my body rival Pompeii for a day.
Just do anything. Please.
There are only so many times
I can call out your name,
before it begins to sound like a death sentence

MADE FOR PLASTIC CUPS

I wanted to tell you something beautiful today,
but I didn't get to hear your voice.
That is sadly becoming a pattern as of late.
Life keeps giving us more than we can handle,
and conveniently forgetting to leave the receipt
upon our respective dressers.
But we'll make do,
and we'll keep the darkness at bay.
We don't have much of a choice,
we're just wired that way.
But darling, what I wanted to tell you is this... I miss you.
I miss you terribly.
No hyperbole. No exaggeration.
Just truth. Keeping the promise I made to you.
And the truth is,
I feel lost when I don't hear from you.
And I'm sorry if I overwhelm you
with my affection, babe.
I have a bad habit of hiding oceans behind my eyes,
and then trying to fit waterfalls into plastic cups.
The poor things weren't made to handle all of this.
But I feel as though you were made for me.
And I have waited thirty-something years
for someone as incredible as you.
Yet, I feel as though
you are slipping through my fingers,
and I only want to hold you
for as long as I've waited for you.
Is that so much to ask?
I've never been this close to glory before.
I need to know if you really exist.
Because you're starting to feel like
a figment of my cruel imagination.

CLYDE HURLSTON

A KING MADE TO KNEEL

Writer's envy often takes
my mind to dark places.
I read the words of others,
and it literally pains me
that I haven't said those things to you.
I want to shout these things from mountaintops.
But the blank page is all I have.
And I know there are some things
the world can never know.
But darling, I want to tell them how your name
has become a mantra that brings me peace.
I can meditate and lose myself in daydreams.
Picturing all of the wonderful things
I would do for you.
Expecting nothing in return but that smile.
My god, that smile.
It's the one thing that can turn a King into a beggar.
For I would let my knees make love to the ground,
only if it would make you happy.
I only want to love you, baby. That's it.
Everyday for the rest of your days.
With each tomorrow bringing a chance
to earn the love you gave me the day before.
So that you would know,
deep in your bones, the following:
Your happiness? My drug.
Your eyes? My mirror.
Your smile? My prize.
Your mind? My treasure.
Your heart? My home.
Your soul? My light.
Your Garden? My Heaven.
Your hands? My medicine.

THE SACRED GIFT OF FIRE

Your lips? My wine.
Your grace? My salvation.
You have no idea what you mean to me.
But I swear
to whatever gods there may have been,
I won't stop writing until you do.
You are my everything.
And I need you to know that.

CLYDE HURLSTON

IMPATIENCE IS A VIRTUE

On the cusp of dreams, I wait.
Ever impatient.
Drowning my sorrows in a chalice unseen.
Oh, my tongue has become voracious in its lust.
Waiting, to me, is now akin to torture.
A suffering the silent must endure
if they are to be rewarded.
For haste is the hallmark of fools.
And patience is the weapon of the masters.
Yet here I lay,
somewhere in the middle of the spectrum.
Counting the seconds until she is mine again.
I pace back and forth,
in a cage that does not exist, and I hunger.
Surely biding my time,
and reenacting her martyrdom in my mind
at least a thousand times.
Passion has taken me again.
She has no idea what she does to me.
But then again, her smile says she knows all too well.

ANCHORS

I would drive clear across town
for just a little taste.
She would only need to say the word,
and not a second would waste.
'Cause when someone is in your veins,
all it takes is a little time.
And reason goes out the window,
right along with rhyme.
And I'm proud to say I'm crazy,
always in the mood to play.
This girl slipped her anchors in my bones,
to make sure I never get away.
Mission accomplished darling,
I am yours until the shepherd lifts the veil.
I maybe the captain in my mind,
but it's you that puts the wind inside my sail.
So tell me, where do we go from here?

CLYDE HURLSTON

DEVOUR

Sometimes
No matter how hard you try,
You just can't get your mind out of the gutter.
And honestly, when it comes to you,
I don't really want to.
I want to keep you there.
With makeup smeared, and dirty knees
Looking up at me.
Waiting for me to come down there
And devour you...

LEGENDS

There I go again.
Setting sail upon the high seas of imagination.
Seduced by the tall tales that souls will tell.
Legends of a treasure lost long ago.
Waiting for the worthy to navigate the path
and claim it for their own.
And here I am, howling from the wheelhouse,
hoping I am the one.
Though I'm blinded
by a potent combination of lust and excitement,
I am humbled by the thought of my prize.
My hands, aching to feel the glory I've imagined.
My lips, fighting to keep my breath at bay.
And I ask myself, "Could today be the day?"
And then I see her,
and I know for certain, the legends are for real.

CLYDE HURLSTON

ACROSS THE PLAINS

Deep in the wilderness of my mind,
we bear witness as anticipation reigns.
Desire is the king of all the beasts,
being feared across the plains.
Every other thought that wanders stray,
is blindsided and devoured.
And sadly, it's not just the body count,
that keeps growing by the hour.
Concentration here is rare,
much like storm clouds overhead.
For the heat just inspires thirst,
just like when she is in my bed.
And so there's no escape for modest thoughts,
they'll find no solace in the shade.
For when the beast is drunk on lust,
inhibitions will lead decorum to an early grave.
So I'd suggest these thoughts
had better get on board,
before they're introduced to teeth.
And they have no time to cry for help,
when it's His Majesty
they're pinned and trapped beneath.
So when the King is on the prowl,
may the timid find the floor.
And when she reads my latest roar,
let her know that yes, I am demanding more.

LATE NIGHT CONJURING

She came to me in a dream.
Her hair, the color of fire.
Whispering,
"I've heard your every cry,
Read your every unsaid desire.
I am here to heal your wounds,
And to drain you of your love.
So come lay down beside me now,
And I will show you how."
It is was then I wondered,
"Is this the Goddess,
That my subconscious has conjured?"

CLYDE HURLSTON

CHASING VAPORS

It was late at night
that she became my high.
Strung out in an empty bed.
Chasing vapors behind my eyes,
Down the rabbit hole inside my head.
Fuck, she is incredible.
What she did in minutes,
It took others years to discover.
Without a whisper, without a touch.
Only with her written words.
That is how she stoked this desire.
Causing me to burn,
as her personal funeral pyre.
Now she pretends not to understand.
Oblivious to her own power.
Well, who else put this rhythm in my hand?
Won't you return tonight, darling?
So that I may relapse into bliss again?
And imagine how you'll feel,
the moment I'm finally deep within.

HOWL AT THE MOON

My lips have caressed
your name a thousand times.
Each having tasted better than the last.
And on lonely nights,
I salivate at the very thought of you.
Baby, you must know
by now what you do to me.
I'm here in the darkness,
pacing back and forth.
Counting the times
you've failed to look my way.
Knowing full well you'll pay
for every one of them,
the next time I'm inside you.
The wolf within takes umbrage
with being ignored.
And when I see you glowing in the distance,
I have no choice but to seethe.
For every day without you,
is a day I do not want to breathe.
But still, you make me do just that.
And so, I'm here
doubled over in hunger pains,
since you always leave me Famished.
Now I must put pen to paper in your honor,
hoping you'll hear my written howls at the moon.

CLYDE HURLSTON

SAFE HARBOR

In this year plus of ours,
I made her many promises.
Many of them will be known to no one but us;
but you should know
that I've done my best to keep them all.
I remember telling her that she was safe now.
That she had nothing to worry about,
because no matter what life threw at us,
we would face it together.
Because I knew the waters
of her past had been turbulent.
And yet, I told her
despite the darkness of my depression,
my heart and soul would always be her lighthouse.
And these open arms would never be her prison,
but rather they would be her safe harbor.
So when she tired of swimming,
she could capsize between them,
and I would hold her until the morning.
And thanks would never be needed.
Because that is what you do
when you love someone
more than you love yourself:
you protect them.
And as I lie alone in this bed,
even after all this time,
I still wonder if I shine brightly enough
for her to find her way back home.

THE HEAVY HANDS OF FATE

Darling, has our fire been extinguished?
Or does it smolder just the same?
Are you still ignoring
the smoke in your subconscious?
While mine proudly bathes inside the flame?
Tell me, have you found this silence to be golden?
Have you learned to dance beneath the rain?
Or did the wind stop and change direction?
Causing your sails to fall in shame?
Has this path brought to you adventure?
Or another challenge in its guise?
Have the tears continued falling,
downward from your perfect eyes?
Has a smile now graced your lips,
and become a fixture through the days?
Or has disappointment taken root,
in the fields that joy once used to graze?
Oh, I only wished you to be happy,
never once did I speak of you with hate.
For I knew I would rather struggle with you,
than to leave you alone to face the heavy hands of fate.

CLYDE HURLSTON

NO SERMONS

I've dreamed of you so many times,
I'm surprised it hasn't manifest.
I toss and turn almost every night,
because my desire won't let me rest.
Your face will dance behind my eyes,
before your body makes me beg.
And I imagine how my shoulders look,
as each displays your aching legs.
Darling, you've tantalized my soul for years,
and made me wonder how you'd taste.
But now you'll take me as deep as I can go,
right down to its very base.
'Cause I want to make you cry out for God,
though no sermon has left your lips.
And your fingernails find a home inside the sheets,
as your love pours until it drips.
You know with me you're safe to come undone,
that's why you've provoked the beast.
Since I'm too reserved throughout the day,
you'd choose the night to let me feast.
And as your garden became the sacrament,
your heart remained the Holy Grail.
So my tongue would explore your temple walls,
as if you left instructions raised in Braille.
But then I'd slip deeper into sleep,
before the alarm clock sang its song.
And life would force me to accept the fact,
that you were never mine for long.

STORIED ENDING

To tell you the truth, since she left,
I have often dreamed of her return.
Countless were these slumbering fantasies;
each of a reunion so grand
it would make the clouds stop and take notice.
But I've since come to realize the truth:
that storied ending is just not going to happen.
There is only one end for a flame
which burned that fucking brightly:
it never burns for very long.
And even if she did come back,
there is no way for us to reignite the ashes;
for it was our inhibitions and society's rules
that we once proudly reduced to rubble.
Our only choice now
would be to build something new together,
and ensure that our passions used it as the pyre,
from which our smoke would choke the gods.
But such a thought is better left inside my head.
For she is nowhere to be found, and there is
another who will take her place within my bed.

CLYDE HURLSTON

YOUR RIGHTFUL PLACE

Since there is still
only silence between us,
I write these words
and pray they reach your eyes...
Darling, I truly hope
you live well for the rest of your days.
And I hope your soul
can find comfort in knowing
that there was at least one man in the world,
who never wanted to cause you pain.
No, he would have much preferred
to have bled beside you,
and shared enough love
that both of our wounds could heal in time.
But as it stands now,
you seem content to suffer in solitude;
and whether it is due to pride or guilt,
I will not dare presume to know.
I just hope you know
in your very bones that I am still here;
walking ever so slowly toward the light.
Always letting one hand trail behind me,
in the hopes that you will catch up
and take your rightful place beside me.
For no matter how much it pains me,
I fear I will love you for the rest of your life,
and the rest of my own.

WHEN SHE BECAME THE SUN

Loneliness and desire gave me wings,
Knowing my legs were far too proud to run
As I grew obsessed with morning glory,
For in these eyes, she had become the sun.
So feathers and wax were combined
To make parts equal to their sum
In time, I would blindly fall in love
Just before my wings would come undone
Still, like a fool I flew closer
Thinking she would never let me down
But instead of meeting destiny in the sea
I would prove Daedalus right
When I came crashing to the ground.

CLYDE HURLSTON

AN INTERNAL FIRE

From the peaks we helped each other reach.
I believed I could see Heaven.
That oft-referenced place,
That mirrored what I saw in her eyes.
Yet, no matter what heights we experienced,
Coming back down to Earth
Always felt a bit like Hell.
Because in my heart of hearts I knew,
So much sand would fall within the glass
Before I would get to see her again.
And when I think of her wearing nothing,
My patience would wear thin.
That's when wants breathe the air of needs,
Leaving me stumbling through my days.
Being consumed by an internal fire,
And trying to find her through the haze.

THESE TIRED HANDS

They tell me that it is useless
to try and reach out to me.
The reason being,
they constantly read my words,
and are unceremoniously greeted with the truth:
the potential for new love
simply cannot compete with your memory.
I believe they hate how these tired hands
and these humble lines cry out for you,
as if you were redemption for the repentant.
But they do not understand, my love.
They cannot fathom that for me,
the sun still rises and sets in the blue of your eyes.
For they were the skies,
in which I had first learned to fly.
So they say these things,
because they are blind to the fact
that I do not want to be a King,
if you are not in the throne beside me.
They don't know the pride I feel,
knowing it is your name,
and your name alone,
still emblazoned across my bones.
And I believe it would pain them to discover
that I still live to feel your love.
I would gladly work to share in your happiness.
And without hesitation, I would die to keep you safe.
So what chance could they have to compete with you,
when even my memories fail to do you justice?

CLYDE HURLSTON

THESE PIXELATED FIRES

My eyes pour over the words of others;
hoping, praying even,
that in them I will find a spark.
But alas, the exhaustive searches
have all been for naught
For the flame appears
to have been extinguished
once and for all, dear reader.
I guess without fresh memories
to act as the coal I would feed the blaze;
even the most towering of infernos
grows tired of burning.
And if we are being honest,
who here could blame it?
Where there was once
a serenade of crackling,
there is now only deafening silence.
Where there was once
charring and plumes of smoke
to choke the weak,
there is now only soot on an unused tongue;
the remnants of the lustful words I used to speak.
Hell, I once displayed
these stretch marks as if they were burns;
in the hopes of proudly telling the world,
you had branded me as your own.
But as I lie before this flashing screen,
I am reminded that I will forever be alone.
Because you won't even
point a finger in my direction now;
and my skin aches for the way
you once made it sweat.
Proving that the videos of these pixelated fires,

are not able to help my mind forget.
Instead, they cause me to long for the days,
when I was your favorite of the pyres.

CLYDE HURLSTON

WILL OLD FLAMES RISE?

On my lonely nights,
I would often contemplate
the reasons for your silence.
Had you felt betrayed?
Maybe even offended that other women
usurped your place within my words?
Was there a tinge of envy, knowing that another soul
would discover the joy you knew so well?
Were you angry that I would touch them,
where no man has since been able to reach you?
Tell me, darling,
now that you have returned to me in friendship,
is there an urge to reclaim
what you feel is your rightful place?
Tell me, do these lines
not still feel like fuses in your veins?
Are you not looking for a written spark,
so that what was once an old flame,
may find what it needs to dance again?
For you know damn well the things we used to do;
the heights our fire used to reach!
We were the reason
the bottoms of the clouds were singed.
And I remember days when the gods
sent the world rain, just to cool us off.
And I know you have not forgotten that, my love.
So tell me, has the day finally come
that you have tired of merely existing,
and wish to feel alive again?

HER DEFINITION OF HEAVEN

I once asked her for her definition of Heaven;
and she replied,
"a warm bath and a tall glass of wine."
Given the speed of her response,
I deduced that the water relaxed her body,
as the Moscato relaxed her mind.
For both her patience and her grace
helped her make it through the day;
and now she was dying to unwind.
Ever so slowly,
she must have removed the pins
from her raven-colored hair;
and it came pouring down upon her shoulders;
as if the night formed a waterfall
to drown the daylight.
While she was there soaking and content,
I could imagine her breath
dancing upon her tongue;
as she released that long-drawn sigh.
Steam dancing off her silken skin,
proving that the temperature was just right.
And as her concerns slipped away,
and her cares were submerged
beneath the soapy surface,
I imagine she felt alive again.
So with the thought of her there,
relaxed and nude, my mind began to race.
I asked, "if that's Heaven, baby.
What would make you want to leave it?"
Her reply?
"Knowing you're on your way home,
and aching to punish me properly."

CLYDE HURLSTON

IN A FASHION JUST THE SAME

How long has it been, darling?
Do you even remember the last time
the fires burned so strongly within you,
that you could put your lips together
and exhale plumes of smoke?
Or have the flames
been so dormant in your soul,
that you've forgotten how intense
their roars and crackling sound?
For although it's felt like years
since we were face to face,
I bet I could see the truth inside your eyes.
You wouldn't be able to hide then.
Yet having said that, I need you to know
that I admire the way you step forward with grace;
keeping the world blind to the fact
that you've been falling apart.
Very few know exactly what you've been through;
but thankfully, I do.
And that is why I am here.
To let you know that I can read
between the lines you never wrote,
and I can hear the words you have never spoke.
I know full well those perfect lips
remember how to say my name.
And I can still remember
you wanting me to make your body quiver,
as you took the Lord's in vain.
Darling, I know you won't admit it,
but I bet you still ache for me
in places you cannot reach.
And I know you don't have
to think long and hard

THE SACRED GIFT OF FIRE

about the times your hands
caused my love to stand,
in a fashion just the same.
All you have to do is speak the words,
and I will help you to break free
and reawaken your desires;
one hard thrust at a time.

IMMORTAL LOVE

As long as i live,
I will never forget her.
I am sure she knows this.
For although I could not
control how it ended,
I will control the way
our love is remembered.
She will live forever
between these lines.
For it was my honor
to see her come alive,
knowing she was safe.
Knowing she was loved.
With me, she was free..
To be the goddess she already was.

THE COLLECTED DEBT OF SLEEP

I've fancied myself a king,
and imagined you a queen.
Sharing this entire world as a kingdom,
and living a life serene.
But the truth is with all the ebbs and flows,
I'm not even sure if you're mine.
And if the inferno we are trying to feed,
will really stand the test of time.
But I hope the breath that you take from me,
will help the fire rise.
And light the fuse of the ungodly plans,
that I fight to hide behind my eyes.
And if you would like to know the truths,
that I was reticent to tell.
Then you must now prepare yourself,
before you receive a sample from the well.
For I have lived a lifetime in my days,
and lived days within my dreams.
I've spoken profoundly with my silence,
and yet said nothing with my screams.
I've known opulence at the cost of thoughts,
and succumbed to the collected debt of sleep.
I've grasped at memories like grains of sand,
hoping to contain the information that they keep.
But all of this will simply pale,
when compared to my dark desires.
For i long to be inside of you,
and provide your favorite of the pyres...

CLYDE HURLSTON

THE OVERZEALOUS STUDENT

Darling, I'm an overzealous student;
can't you see my hand is raised?
I know you've read my words;
do you feel you have been praised?
I've poured over every thought,
in my efforts to ensure.
That these things I feel for you,
are both true and pure.
And now you know they are,
so I bid your doubts to rest.
Since I've studied to prepare myself,
for each impending test.
For within your every breath,
is a lesson to be learned.
And I know you are indeed a prize,
that must be truly earned.
So I wish to know your language,
won't you bless this uncertain tongue.
Are there levels to your love?
May I caress each, waiting rung?
Or must I remain forever alone,
praying to one day be called upon?

WEIGHTLESS

In the past,
I felt weightless.
Her love lifted me
To places that only
Telescopes could see.
But now she is gone.
I am lost without my moon.
I am untethered and adrift.
And out here,
Breathing feels like dying.
So now I know exactly
How the sun feels
During an eclipse.
How could I continue
To burn this hot for you,
And still go unseen?

CLYDE HURLSTON

BREATHE LIFE

Darling, for me,
missing you is as easy as breathing.
Yet, the very thought of you,
still takes my breath away.
So won't you return,
and breathe life into the lips
that still proudly bear your name?

GREEN WITH ENVY

Late at night,
I find myself
getting green with envy.
For it is your bed
that has you all to itself,
and not me.
Oh darling,
the things I would do to you
if only I were given the chance.

CLYDE HURLSTON

THE WAY OF THE GODS

Never fill the chalice completely.
For that would simply sate their thirst.
Instead, let them earn each sip.
Teach their perfect lips to ache
for another drop of what you have.
And know that is the way of the gods.

ADVENTURE

Seeing as how
she loved an adventure,
I thought she would come
to appreciate my mind.
But as it turns out,
She would much rather
discover a place
that she didn't already rule.

CLYDE HURLSTON

EFFORTLESS

Darling,
To distill the things
I once felt for you
Into a few lines required effort.
But when you were here,
And when you were willing
You know damn well
That showing you was effortless

AS FREE AS A BIRD

This time was different.
It had been years since I had seen her.
Because of the smoke we produced in the past,
conversations in the present
were always carefully measured;
for we both knew that the fumes still lingered.
So we had best not create any sparks.
Still, it brought me great sadness
to learn of the cage her life had become.
There are few things worse
than seeing a free spirit endure bondage,
without the pleasure that should follow.
So it was no wonder that the locks deep within her
cried out for their master key.
And consequently,
it was no surprise that she returned to me.
She readily admitted that there was no one
who gave her release the way that I did.
With me, her burdens
could be set down and forgotten.
From the first turn of this key,
my confidence was not the only thing that grew.
The fire within her had been relit;
and the flames had reached her eyes.
The cage door had swung open,
and she was once again as free as a bird.

CLYDE HURLSTON

HOURGLASS

I once heard that
closed mouths will never get fed;
and yet I've learned through trial and error,
that open books will never get read.
Because it's things that are discovered
that will become a part of lore,
and it's things that are presented,
that will introduce an interest to a bore.
A man must first strive and forge himself,
into a highly, treasured find.
For there is not a scarcity upon the shelves,
one must be made inside her mind.
And I could tell the world so many things,
layered deep within a rhyme.
But I know she'd rather have me build a watch,
than to simply tell the current time.
Because she knows that men are clocks,
and they rush with overzealous hands.
And so she longs to love an hourglass,
that will always catch its falling sands.
You must let her build her monuments,
where there once was only stones.
And in turn, she'll feel a desire so profound,
it will burn your name into her bones.

LESSONS LEARNED

It always makes me laugh,
the way people judge
inexperienced lovers.
For how can someone
be expected to be fluent
in a language
they have never heard before?
And so for those like me
whom were rarely sought after,
the lessons come few and far between.
But rest assured, I learned them well.
Now the one before me smiles.
Because she is aware
that the way she likes it,
is the way I know how to do it best.

CLYDE HURLSTON

THE INTIMATE JOYS

Darling,
Because I pour myself
into these lines I write,
they are the still waters
that are said to run deep.
And to experience my passion,
one must first be brave.
Showing me, they are willing
to fully submerge themselves
within each piece;
despite the risk of drowning.
Because we all know,
it is the timid soul
that has never known
the intimate joys of getting wet.

WHAT I MISS MOST

Darling.
When the sun goes down
and my thoughts are the heaviest,
do you want to know
what I miss the most?
More than the laughing.
More than the teasing.
More than the hot, passionate sex.
I miss the way your eyes lit up
when you told me you loved me.
I miss the way your lips tasted
after your signature kiss.
God damn it...
What I miss the most is you.

CLYDE HURLSTON

WATER:HER

Water her with love
and watch the way she blooms.
Marvel as she reaches
upward for the sun,
Bestowing us with grace
for many moons.

THE WATERS OF NO OTHER

So many young people nowadays
liken desire to being thirsty.
Well let the record show,
that for her,
I will always remain dry-mouthed.
For my desire to please her
knows no bounds.
She rescued me from drowning
upon dry land.
My tongue now knows
the taste of bliss because of her.
I will drink from her fountain
for as long as she will have me.
I crave the waters
if no other woman but her.
And I pray that I remain baptized
in her love, until the end of all time.

CLYDE HURLSTON

THE MANNER IN WHICH I'VE BURNED

Very rarely is there shame
within these words, darling.
The world now knows
the manner in which I've burned for you.
They've learned how these words
boiled within my veins,
before searing themselves
upon these unsuspecting pages.
How could I ever hope to hide,
that which at times
feels like a burden to carry?
There are but few souls
that know the depths of a love like mine.
And that is the reason why I write.
So that when my days have reached their end,
history will show
that when my love for a woman surfaced,
it left a path no other man could follow.

PLAY THE MOTH

Everyone wants a woman
who has fire in her veins,
until they end up getting burned.
And as a man whom
was once reduced to ashes
in the name of love,
I recognize all of the signals in the smoke..
Still, I can't help but play the moth
to that kind of flame.
Leaving her as living proof,
that we should all
be careful what we wish for.

CLYDE HURLSTON

UPON THESE PAGES

Have you ever stopped to think
That you're immortal now, baby?
That because you've been inside my lines
More often that I've been inside of you,
Generations to come will discover
The times we came together.
And here upon these pages,
Others will be able to read
of the literal love we made.
Their eyes will pour across
The lines that speak of my every thrust,
And your every gasp,
As I reached the edges of your soul.
Yes darling, upon these pages
Others will come to learn,
About the greatest moments I have known.
My only wish,
Is that our time together
Would have lasted just as long.

THE FIRST AMONG MANY

With enough time to think,
Almost anything can be justified.
And when it came to her,
I had convinced myself
That there was something
sacred about the wait.
That if I showed enough want,
Enough ache
She would see my reverence for our union.
Because she once saw me as royalty,
I believed that she would appreciate my loyalty.
For I wanted no other lover but her.
But now I have learned the truth:
No woman wants a man without options.
No woman wants to remain
With a man who has no other place to go.
They want that which others want
But simply cannot have.
They want to be chosen; never relied upon.
For when it comes to love,
Wants and needs are a part of the game.
But in her eyes,
My wanting all or nothing
Reeks of desperation all the fucking same.

CLYDE HURLSTON

SEE THE FIRE

My fingers trace your every photograph,
While wishing it was your skin.
But it seems there's nothing that I possess,
That would cause you to let me in.
Maybe it's the way I look,
Or maybe it's how much I weigh.
Maybe it's because I don't play hard to get,
Or even push you away.
Maybe I notice too many little things,
You wish were overlooked.
And here I've never had a taste of you,
So how do you have me hooked?
Oh, I wish I could change the way I felt,
Just so I'd never play the fool.
Yet I seem to be the kind of soul,
For which you're always making rules.
Because I'm not the type to really make a move
Unless given permission along the way.
And I fear I'm honest to a fault,
So I don't hesitate before I say:
When I see you smile it gives me hope,
That the darkness won't always win.
And sometimes you look so fucking good.
My every thought becomes a sin.
And I don't apologize for wanting you,
Since closed mouths are never fed.
But I know the only way that you'll be mine,
Is here inside my head.
For I'll never be the one you lie beside,
Since I'm missing what you desire.
Still, it's torture knowing that I burn for you,
And you don't even see the fire.

WAKE THE BEAST

She always knows exactly what to do,
when she wants to get me going.
Just flash a certain look,
a slight turn of phrase,
and she might as well be
striking stones together.
Because it won't be long
before the fire starts.
And when it does,
she knows the smoke we produce
is what will surely wake the beast.

CLYDE HURLSTON

MADE TO FORGET

Over the years I've learned
that there will be times
when she simply
wants me to sit and listen,
as she explains
what's wrong in her world.
And I've also learned,
there will be times
when she wants to be
pinned against the wall
and made to forget
the outside world exists.
Though I've felt it was
my duty as a man
to know which
she needed before she spoke:
I've since come to realize
that it is her that knows herself the best.
So she will let me know
when she needs either option.
And because I love her, I'll be ready.

THE DEVIL IN ME

It has long been said
that fortune favors the bold.
So in my mind,
that means timidity
has no place here
in our respective journeys
around the sun.
For whether it is through
the grace of my pen,
or the firmness of my love,
it is your reaction, darling,
that brings out the devil in me.
And no matter what the gods will say,
I know they take delight
in watching me behave this way.
Because with each act I finish,
it is your perfect lips
that end up calling out their names.

CLYDE HURLSTON

HIDING THE MOON

You'd swear I hid the moon in my words,
as much as she howled my name
when reading them.
It's as if a turn of phrase was all it took,
and there was no longer a lady to be found.
Rather she was but a wolf within a dress;
dying to unleash her primal side.
But in truth, there's more
to her transformation than that.
For I am well aware
that there is an undeniable power
in reading the words
you've always wanted to hear.
Knowing their writer
holds your remedy within their hands,
as they create without an ounce of fear.
I know damn well
what I do to you with these lines, darling.
It's the same thing you do to me
with just a look.
So go on...
howl for me, baby.
Let me know exactly where you need it.

MY CHURCH HAS A NAME

My church, she has a name.
A sobriquet I'm not inclined to share.
For she is the holiest of places;
a space far beyond compare.
Yet if I were to tell you,
my worthiness would be lost.
And I'd then be forced to pay,
much too high a cost.
For I was cast down and out of Eden,
long before my birth.
And I have searched and searched for her,
since my feet first touched the Earth.
Now she lies beside me,
each time my eyes are closed.
And being this close to Heaven,
makes it hard to stay composed.
So as my pulse begins to race,
more than desire begins to rise.
As it becomes more visible,
she can't believe her eyes.
So she places her hand upon a love,
that she hardened with a glance.
Then she helps me take it out,
and so begins the dance.

CLYDE HURLSTON

NO INTENTIONS

She once asked me,
"Why do you love me so much?"
And I said,
"Because on days that I feel like Popeye,
you are my spinach.
And on days I feel like Superman,
you are my kryptonite."
She put her hand over her perfect lips,
trying to hide her laughter, while saying
"Well, I guess you better hold on to me then."
And before she could say anything else,
I started to lift her
off the ground as I kissed her.
Because I had no intentions
of ever letting her go.

THE ONLY WAYS I KNOW

It pains me when I think about it, darling.
What you've been settling for
these last few years.
I mean, don't get me wrong,
I know women like you
will always make the best of a bad situation.
But let's not mince words here, love:
You're overworked and far too underpaid.
And then you get home,
and you aren't even properly laid.
I know you're taken for granted everyday,
but when was the last time
you were taken from behind?
You don't even have to tell me, baby.
I know that you're overdue for satisfaction.
Hell, I bet if I were to look
into your eyes right now,
I wouldn't even see the spark
that used to start the fires in me.
But that's okay, darling.
Because we're going to rekindle the flames
and burn together.
And despite being out of practice,
you needn't worry.
For I haven't forgotten a single fucking thing.
All the ways you like it done,
are still the only ways I know.

CLYDE HURLSTON

A WORLD INSIDE

There lies a world inside of me.
A place where I have hidden the things
I didn't want others to see.
Emotions and desires
that I didn't want to believe were a part of me.
But she sensed there was far more
to me than what was
displayed on my imperfect surface.
She was not afraid of
what she couldn't see.
In fact, she was only afraid of
not discovering everything.
And that's when she took me by the hand,
and began to show me
what I had been missing.
It once was said that in hell,
it is dark and hot.
So she decided to put her halo away,
just to help me keep it that way.

WITHOUT WORRY

Darling, give yourself to me
Without worry.
For behind my doors,
There are no judgments
Waiting for you.
Only profound pleasures
Laced with a little pain.
Just the way you like it.
Here our demons can
Come out and play together;
As they watch
The ungodly things
We will do to one another.

CLYDE HURLSTON

FINDING EXCUSES

I've reached the age,
Where my first thoughts
Are usually cynical ones.
But all of that changed
When I saw her.
My God, she was gorgeous.
I tried my very best
Not to stare at her;
But I couldn't stop myself
From finding excuses
To look in her direction.
It was as if
A star was exploding
Before my eyes.
I couldn't find
The words to speak.
I simply watched
As beauty went supernova
And blew my fucking mind.

BLINDSPOT

This world has so many rules:
A man should do this;
But he should never do that.
And the list goes on and on.
But while I agree
That frames should be maintained
Sometimes things aren't
So easy to control.
Because if I have one
Single blindspot in life,
It is her.
That is where
Her thrones resides.
And when she sits before me
In all of her glory,
And my monument is raised,
It is clear
That her plan is working.

CLYDE HURLSTON

A POSTCARD OF SORTS

There are so many places in this world
That I wish to see
Before I join the ancestors.
However,
Being a man of modest means,
It is difficult for me to travel.
I often see wonders
Only in my imagination.
So she decided to change that.
Knowing i've been losing my battle
With the darkness as of late,
She wanted to remind me
That I was desired.
That the voice in my head was lying.
So she sent me a postcard of sorts.
A picture of the place
Below her shapely waist,
I call my paradise.
And she signed it:
"I wish you were here."

EQUAL PARTS

She is equal parts angel,
equal parts devil.
And she is a snake charmer to boot.
Her feminine wiles are more potent now,
than when she was in her youth.
She is the place
where dreams and fantasies,
are said to come alive.
She is the muse I have been waiting for,
and so clearly been denied.

CLYDE HURLSTON

SKILLED PENS, FLAMING HEARTS

I've lost count of the nights
I have pictured you behind my eyes, love.
Hell, I've already used this pen and told you
about the fabled Rhythm In My Hand.
I have written time and time again,
proudly explaining my Rituals Of Loneliness.
I have typed up my smoke-filled dreams
and I have verbally recalled profanity-laced fantasies.
Each time, the silence only grew louder.
Each time, I waited;
hoping that the ink you found between these lines
wouldn't be the only thing that was wet.
Yet, you seem impervious to my charms.
And yet, you've proven your eyes immune,
to these written pictures that I paint
and display for the world to see.
I wonder if they think me strange…
For holding this flaming heart outstretched,
in attempts to warm you
in places you cannot reach.
And all I've learned to do,
is accept this humility,
your departure has sought to teach.
But I never will regret,
my constant burning in this way.
When so many have been reduced to ash,
and never had lips as skilled as yours,
to ever blow them away.

DETRIMENTAL TO FIRE

I was admittedly
Unprepared for her arrival.
A gift born in moments;
The welcomed product
Of a most casual curiosity.
And Heaven help me,
I knew nothing
Of the many layers she contained.
But I have spent
The subsequent years,
Trying my very best
To unravel her mysteries.
Hoping, even if it was in vain,
That I might make my way
To the center of her labyrinth.
But still, she hides things from me.
And I know that for women
As passionate as her
Attraction is something that will wane.
It is a paradox
I have been unable to reconcile.
Because I burn for her
As brightly as I ever did,
Yet I am not always the spark
That causes the inferno within her.
Leaving me to wonder,
If it's time or distance,
That is the most detrimental to fire..

CLYDE HURLSTON

HER WORDS, NOT MINE

I always thought that
she gave me too much credit.
Demanding that I take the blame for things
I had no idea I was doing.
You see, she would often drop hints
as to what she considered my "crimes."
Said in the most playful sense of the word.
Yet she would never directly answer my questions.
Eventually, she let the the truth
slip out of her perfect lips one day,
when we were in casual conversation.
She would go on to infer
that when my hands moved
to write these erotic words,
that they may as well
have been rubbing sticks together.
Because I would start a fire in her,
and not have the decency
to be there and put it out.
Thankfully, I always left her wet enough,
that her hands never got burned
when she touched herself.
And for the record, those were her words, not mine.

A SIREN'S SONG

It's not that I was anything close to a master...
Truth be told, I lacked the experience
to even be considered well-versed
in ways of helping her to make music.
But what I lacked in repetition,
I made up for
with sheer passion and persistence.
You see, I studied her.
While others were focused
on stresses or trivialities,
I was enthralled with her
and her every move.
For I wanted to know
all the ways she could be pleased.
I longed to discover every angle
from which she could be given ecstasy.
And I was aching to unravel
the depths of her needs,
as soon as I made it past
the peaks of her wants.
Is it any surprise then,
that my siren serenades me
with her hypnotic song
of prolonged moans and exasperated gasps?

CLYDE HURLSTON

DEEP ENOUGH TO DROWN

Through no fault of my own,
These pictures I paint with ink,
Were known to make her wet.
And as I got to know her better
I began to view her
As living proof
That still waters do indeed run deep.
And when I looked at her,
My God... I wanted to go
Deep enough to fucking drown..

CONJURING LOVE

Who knew, after all of this time,
that my Rituals Of Loneliness had worked?
Who knew I had the power to conjure
an untamed woman such as her?
For I never dreamed that the motions of my wrist
could free her from the bondage of inhibitions.
I had foolishly believed myself
to be without a chance to engage in such a dance.
And once again,
the gods have sought to prove me wrong.
For she gave herself unto me,
without hesitation.
And thus, I write of her without end.
I love her without ego.
And when she needs it,
I pleasure her without mercy.

CLYDE HURLSTON

THE LAND OF OUR ANCESTORS

What is it about you, darling?
How have you come to fascinate me so?
It is more than just your beauty.
It is more than just your mystery.
You have captured my imagination.
Just as Egypt did when I was but a child.
And yet today I am a man,
and it continues to haunt
my very thoughts and dreams.
Similar to the way that you do;
in a fashion all the same.
And given the chance,
I would not only journey to Egypt,
but I would painstakingly explore
every single inch of your temple, love.
But sadly, you do not belong to me.
So you are out of my reach.
Just like the land of our ancestors.

DEFIANT; EVEN IN DOUBT.

Darling, I must admit,
it is easy for me to see why I have not
become a household name in this world.
For I have never been the best at anything.
I am not the best-looking,
certainly not the best-dressed.
I am not the best athlete,
and I couldn't carry a tune to save my life.
I have experienced only humble blessings
and never the finer things in life.
Hell, despite how many times
I've written about you in the past,
I am not even the best writer.
But even with all of this time that has passed,
what I do know, and what I'll go to my grave believing,
is that I was the very best at loving you.
And there is not a fucking soul on this Earth,
that can tell me otherwise.
Not even you.

CLYDE HURLSTON

RECITING ROYAL DEMANDS

My days of seeking to unravel riddles are over.
Speak plainly, my love.
Tell me what you need.
Tell me what you crave.
Give yourself to me,
and I will love you until I see the grave.
I know of no other way to love,
I have said it many times.
And I have told this wretched world of you,
in far too many rhymes.
Yet here I am with pen again,
reciting royal demands.
And I've still yet to find your body here,
in these worn but eager hands.
But beside me there lies a waiting throne,
on which you should take your rightful place.
But that's when you're not sitting upon my face,
or taking my hardened love right up to its base.

THE MOON WAS MINE

She came to me at a time
when my world was at its darkest;
requiring nothing from me.
Only wanting to give, love and light.
And she has found her way
between these lines so many times,
seeing as she brought me back to life.
I guess, in the end, that's why
it's been so hard to let her go.
When you love someone so much,
that something as simple
as sharing breath with them gets you high,
all you want to do is inhale.
But eventually, for the sake of balance,
everything must be exhaled.
And deep down, my heart knows it to be true.
For the moon belongs inside the sky.
Some days, I still can't believe she was mine.
Even if only for a while.
Still, I often ask myself:
"Am I wrong to want her back?"

CLYDE HURLSTON

WHAT GOES UNSEEN

I see you lying there, my love.
Your frustrations overwhelming you.
With full lips pouted in protest.
Yes, I see you lying there,
like the still waters of lore.
Running far deeper than most men dare to dip;
or ever dare to drink.
But you must move, my love.
For if given enough time,
even still water becomes stagnant.
Capable of doing far more harm than good.
And I will not allow this for you.
Not after all you have done for me.
So it is after the softest kiss,
I must bludgeon you with truth.
The current state of your days is your own doing.
But the undoing of them will be mine.
So now that I have kissed you again,
I ask you now to use that perfect mouth of yours.
Receive this offering before you.
And together, we shall sing a song
none will dare to cover.
For that which goes unseen,
is usually felt the hardest.
Is it not?

MATTERS OF THE MOON

I've sought to understand your darkness
But received only silence back instead
I've tried my best to aid your fighting
With the demons in your head
But now I've come to realize
That help is far from what you seek
Yet that is another assumption made
Since you refuse to speak
Darling, I fear you mistake my zeal with aid
As a failed acknowledgment of strength
So your preferred unit of measurement
Becomes an arm and all its length
Still, I often try and try again in vain
Hoping you'll respect my unwillingness to yield
But when it comes to matters beneath the moon
The heart is just another weapon that you'll wield.

CLYDE HURLSTON

IT PAINS ME TO KNOW

It pains me to know
That you exist in this world;
and yet you are not mine.
Although you were once.
For a small duration of time.
No one penetrated your voracious mind
or your welcoming body
as deeply as I did, my love.
Still, you chose to run from a union
as powerful as ours.
Convincing yourself that it was easier
to settle for what was near,
despite knowing my intentions
were displayed and crystal clear.
God, what I wouldn't give for one chance
to take you past the number five.
Since you won't give me forever.

SYMPHONIES

Can I be honest with you?
I don't know how much I can take.
The mystery is killing me.
I need to know how you feel, darling.
Daydreams wear off too quickly,
and I need a prolonged high.
I need you to see,
that more than seas will rise,
once this storm comes rolling in.
I need to hear the symphonies,
you hold within your breath.
As the beast within me,
pounds your shores like the tide.
There will be no erosions here, baby.
Just explosions.
My fuse was lit the first time you looked at me.
So what are you waiting for?
And she said, "that'll do it."

CLYDE HURLSTON

THE LENGTHS I'D GO

I have burned for those whom never learned.
I have bled for those
whom rarely turned their head.
My heart broke, as they continued leaving
and never spoke.
And I have cried for those whom
would have never known if I had died.
So could you just imagine,
what I would do for the soul
that felt the same way about me?
My God, the lengths I would go,
just to be met halfway by someone.

THE LITTLE THINGS

If you asked me what I missed the most about her,
I could probably write you a book.
Shit, I already have,
if you've read between the lines.
Still, when I think back,
it's not just the intensity and passion that I miss;
no, that goes without saying.
But what seems to have left the largest void,
were the little things...
The playful teasing.
The inside jokes.
The phrases that no one understood but us.
The ones that acted like
combinations for the locks inside of us.
The getting each other started,
in places we couldn't finish.
My God, what I wouldn't give
to have that again in my life.

CLYDE HURLSTON

THE LANGUAGE OF LOVE

In all this time I have spent without her,
I have come to find that loneliness
has truly been a teacher filled with wisdom
For it has taught me
that the kiss is the diacritic of the language of love.
It is something so small,
that people will often overlook it;
and most will take it for granted.
But for those whom are fluent in its expression?
Few things matter more.
That is why I miss her perfect lips upon mine.
For it was in those moments,
that salvation came with a hint of saliva.
Yes, it was in those moments
that the warmth of her tongue,
brought with it, a sense of hope.
And it was the shortness of her breath
that truly proved to me,
I was not the only hungry and impatient soul
who longed to be kissed right out of their senses.

TO STUDY HER IS TO LOVE HER

She is a world unto herself;
an endless landscape
and labyrinth all rolled into one.
Yet, for all of her complexities,
it's the little things that bear the most weight.
For they remind her
how much she is loved.
For her, important dates are more than numbers;
they are windows to memories she never wants to lose.
For her, it's not the subtle change
in her appearance that matters most;
but the fact that you studied her enough to notice.
My friend, she wants you to know her.
She wants you to know whether
her sighs were inspired by frustration or exhaustion.
She wants you to know,
that a kiss on the lips shows desire;
but a kiss on the forehead shows her true love.
She wants to know that you have measured
the space between your arms,
and have decided that she fits there just right;
and so you hug her from behind.
She wants to know that, for you,
seeing her is the highlight of your day.
Friend, this world can be a hell;
don't you think it's time that you reminded her,
that she is Heaven on this Earth?

CLYDE HURLSTON

THE SACRED GIFT OF FIRE

END OF ACT I

"Sexual energy comes into play before sex even takes place. The greatest pleasure isn't sex, but the passion with which it is practiced."

- Paulo Coelho

"Real intimacy is a sacred experience. It never exposes its secret trust and belonging to the voyeuristic eye of a neon culture. Real intimacy is of the soul, and the soul is reserved."

- John O'Donohue

ACT II
SACRED TOUCH, SACRED TASTE

"I remember that feeling of skin. It's strange to remember touch more than thought. But my fingers still tingle with it."

- Lucy Christopher

"I taste her and realize I have been starving."

- Jodi Picoult

CLYDE HURLSTON

"The Safety Of Embrace" Art by Sir Render

APPLE OF MY EYE

Since that day in the garden,
women have been blamed
for the downfall of men.
Whether it was Lilith
or her replacement, Eve.
And let's not forget the cursed
like Pandora or Cassandra.
Throughout time,
the fairer have been blamed
for all the ills of this world.
But what of her then?
This forbidden apple of my eye?
Am I to be cursed with expulsion
if I were to succumb to her touch?
Would I know the fires of damnation,
for becoming acquainted with her taste?
Take this truth as a confession, for I do not care.
Whether her halo hides horns, it matters not.
She is an angel that has saved me
from the hell within myself.
And if that earns my place amongst the fallen,
then I bid them to make room within the flames.
Because my list of regrets
shall never know her name.
But these four walls will hear her call mine.
Not in vain,
but from the most delightful sort of pain.

CLYDE HURLSTON

THE MONSTER I BECAME

I'm not like most men, darling.
I am quiet. Reserved.
The animal behind my eyes
only claws its way out when provoked.
You have nothing to fear from me.
I have told you countless times,
I am not the source of your pain.
I am the one who wants to remind you
that your scars will heal.
I am here. Patiently waiting.
Just in the corner of your eye.
Waiting to be seen.
And I would like you to know...
I am not needy for your attention, darling...
I am greedy for it.
Every gaze in my direction is devoured,
Every kind word is inhaled,
Until I am face to face with clouds.
Every smile illuminates
the blackest corners of my mind.
And it is there, the desire grows.
Like vines across the walls of my thoughts.
Filling every nanosecond of silence
with the shape of your name.
The name that lovingly hangs on my tongue
like a family photograph.
I swallow that name whole.
For it is she, and she alone that is to blame.
For this poetic monster that I became.
Feeding... Bleeding on the page.
Pacing... Waiting in the wings.
Trying to unlock this metaphoric cage.
Let me out my love...
I am dying to taste you!

FOOTPRINTS

All of my life, I have been alone.
Living life only within my dreams.
Having been intimate with isolation,
as if I was floating aimlessly in space;
And yet, I have never left the ground.
And so despair became the gravity
I could not escape.
But then you came along.
And never in a million years,
would I think a woman that looks like you,
would look at me the way that you do.
Never in a thousand days,
would I dream that those three words
could ever be intended for me,
from lips as intoxicating as yours,
And what you have proven;
in what seems like
a hundred, different ways,
is that I was wrong.
And I am delighted to be.
So how can I ever repay you?
Ever since you first kissed me,
I've felt like the reason why
there are footprints on the moon.
And to tell you the truth,
I've yet to come down.

FAMISHED

There is a thought
consuming me in this moment.
Gnawing at my eyes
as if it is dying for attention.
And like always, it is her.
The way she lies upon the bed.
Ever motionless, but so alive.
Her hip rising from the sheets,
like the hills in Wicklow.
And I am silent.
Dying to journey
into the valley hidden by the satin.
I so badly want a taste.
But how do you wake an angel when she sleeps?
Is there a polite way to say,
"I hunger for you
and dreams only leave me famished?"
But no, there's not.
And so, I taste her like there's no tomorrow.
And judging from her hands in my hair,
along with that breathtaking arch in her back...
I don't think she minds.

TRANSFERENCE OF POWER

As we sat in my parked car,
she eagerly tugged at my jeans
and asked her question:
"So tell me, baby... do you have a name for it?"
To which I replied, "I do, actually."
"Well... What is it?',
she impatiently quipped
while pointing out my belt was already undone.
"I call it: The Sword In The Stone."
"Why?", she asked;
as her perfect eyes widened with curiosity.
"Because it often goes years
without being touched by another soul;
yet every once in awhile,
someone worthy comes along
and is able to pull it out."
A mischievous smile poured across her lips,
as she took it in her hand and
marveled at what was now hers
as she mused,
"I guess this really does make me your Queen..."
"You're goddamn right it does, baby,"
I said before kissing her so deeply
I could taste her joy.
Then I whispered in her ear, "Now show me
what you're going to do with all your power."
"I'll do better than that," she said.
"I'll show you where I can put all of this..."
And as she takes a sharp inhale of breath,
the gods will bear witness
as a King fast becomes a slave.

CLYDE HURLSTON

ACCIDENTAL FIRES

She gets me started without effort.
She swears that she is not trying to do so,
but I look down and the result
is clearly visible all the same.
Yet I cannot fault the one
who chooses not to stoke
these accidental fires;
for even the wildest of desires
can be controlled.
But having said that,
tonight I do not want to control anything.
When it gets this late,
I have no choice but to remove the sword
and allow myself to burn.
Because when she is my muse,
she puts the movement in my wrist.
And that smile of hers
lets me know that she knows,
writing is not the only release
through which I find peace.

DOWN TO THE LAST DROP

I'm beginning to feel that all too familiar rush;
the unmistakable urge
that not many can understand.
My mind begins to race,
seemingly at a mile per minute.
My palms begin to sweat just a bit;
and my mouth is so dry,
it would surely kill for a drink.
And that can only mean one thing:
it's time for me to reach for her...
the only lover I have.
Unable to resist anymore,
I lift her up and lay her out across my desk.
With the way she unfolds,
she seems to be as impatient as I am.
So I reach into my jeans and remove
the instrument she's been waiting to feel.
The blank look upon her face,
tells me she's been needing this as much as I have.
I try to follow each of her lines,
but I'm too out of control.
My hands are unsteady and my knees are weak;
and I'm crying out to tell the world about her:
my perfect, blank page.
The only place where I can safely explode
and release all that I've been holding inside.
And she takes all of it;
down to the very last drop of ink.

CLYDE HURLSTON

STARLIGHT

Oh, what I wouldn't give
to feel her warm embrace again.
To truly become reacquainted
with the divine touch
that once brought me peace.
Oh, if only I could taste
her perfect lips again.
To allow myself to get drunk
on the anticipation between each kiss.
Discovering that her signature
was still as potent as ever.
Oh, what I wouldn't give
to make love to her again;
if only for one last time.
Just so she could take me
to the farthest corners of outer space,
all from the safety of our bed.
Oh friend, if you asked me what I would give,
I would proudly tell you anything.
Yet those days, and these words,
are just like starlight.
By the time they finally reach your eyes,
it is far too late to change their fate.
And so, like them, I burn alone in the darkness.

A MANIFESTED DREAM

As a few strands of her hair
fell slowly into her face,
she couldn't understand
my obvious reticence to move them.
There have been at least a thousand times,
where I have imagined my hand reaching up
and gently moving them behind her ear.
She smiled as I confessed this,
because she knows exactly
what she does to me with just a look.
And yet, she still cannot fathom
what makes her so special.
"You don't understand, darling.
Because in your mind, you're just you.
But here? In my mind?
Oh fuck baby, you are YOU.
Imagine the grandeur of the universe
being distilled down
into a living form that you could touch.
Now imagine that form
was sitting right next to you,
could actually see you,
and was asking you about itself!
Now do you see why it is so hard for me
to breathe when you look at me?
How does one speak to a manifested dream?
How does one explain matters of the heart,
when it won't stop skipping beats?"
That's when she looked me in the eyes
and whispered, "You don't. You just kiss me."

CLYDE HURLSTON

THE ONLY GIFT

They say today is my day.
The anniversary of my birth.
Another successful trip around the sun.
I am both humbled and grateful.
For I am blessed
to have my senses and my health.
And as I sit here,
surrounded by my closest friends
I have good food in my rather large stomach.
I have a roof over my head,
And clean clothes upon my back.
So compared to some in this world,
I am rich beyond measure.
But there is a thought gnawing
at the back of my mind.
Constantly reminding me of what I don't have.
Knowing that that deep down,
On a day like today, or everyday for that matter
The only gift I want to hold is her.
The only gift I'd wish to taste is her.
The only gift I am dying to unwrap is her.
I wonder if she knows how impatiently I'm waiting?

YOUR FAVORITE BOOK

It pains me to know
that I no longer have the effect
on you that I once did, darling.
You see,
I used to imagine you lying in your bed.
Reading the words
I would share with the world;
with you as their most glorious subject.
Telling them exactly how you made me feel,
and proudly describing
the ungodly things we did to each other.
I would envision the rush of pride you would feel,
knowing that other women
would read those words,
and wish they could be
immortalized in a similar fashion.
And I'll confess, that my ego
was not the only thing that grew,
as I pictured you reliving the memories
I so passionately transcribed.
Darling, in my mind's eye,
I could see you with your head tilted back.
Your phone in your left hand,
and your right hand
hidden beneath the sheets;
as if gently turning the pages
in your favorite book.
I believed you slowly found
what I had left for you between the lines.
And as your hand regained its rhythm,
it was the muse to once again
put this motion in my wrist.
Allowing us to write our stories alone;

CLYDE HURLSTON

until we could be reunited.
But now I fear, these words
no longer cause your hands to move.
What once was hidden between these lines,
no longer seems to ignite
the places you could not reach.
And it breaks my heart to know,
that the pen no longer draws you to the sword.

MY FAVORITE MEAL

Darling, I wanted to apologize for last night.
But the more I thought about it,
I no longer wish to do so.
Because I honestly do not regret
a single thing I feel;
even if it is hunger.
You see, I am a man that has found himself
constantly starved by each missed chance
and a cavalcade of chaotic circumstances.
And when the pains of hunger set in,
I find myself craving my favorite meal:
the greatest thing I have ever tasted
in the entirety of my life;
and that, my love, is you.
And last night, I reached out to you
because I could feel the beast behind my eyes
becoming dangerously impatient.
It began demanding anything from you,
even if it was just a morsel.
And given the way you responded,
I could tell its appetite
was not the only thing that would grow.
Now darling, I know that you have
far too much going on in your life
to allow yourself to be
the main course within this castle;
but ever since this tongue
developed a taste for you,
we both know that nothing else will do.
So I have no choice
but to fast until you can be mine again;
which I beg the gods, will be soon.
And when that day comes baby,
you had best clear your schedule,
and prepare yourself to be devoured without mercy.

CLYDE HURLSTON

CANNON FIRE

I remember every detail vividly, darling...
The mischievous smirk
that poured across your perfect lips,
as I realized what you had in store for me.
The obvious impatience in your gentle hands,
as you undid both my belt and zipper with haste.
The subtle intensity as you stared into my lonely eyes,
as you withdrew my sword from its stone
and began to expertly handle it.
And then the sharp inhale of breath that you drew,
before you finally took me inside of your mouth.
Oh God, baby. It's about time.
You knew I had been waiting weeks for this.
Waiting weeks for you.
To return and use the mouth
that made my name sound like music,
and take me to places
that the scientists have yet to discover.
You took me out of this world,
all from the comfort of my front seat.
My right hand full of your hair,
because you love it when I watched you work.
Fuck, baby.
You then made my body raise off the seat
as the tide of my love began to rise.
And so you went faster and faster,
ensuring your King would explode for you,
in the fashion of cannon fire.

RITUALS OF LONELINESS

Listen as your name is fast repeated,
like incantations for a spell.
And the sweat produced in efforts,
prove the intent to cast them well.
Hands are deliberate with their movements,
in attempts to conjure your return.
But when the monument is raised,
there is no doubt the fire retains its' burn.
Still, you offer the sorcerer only silence,
as if you were the moon in a defiant phase.
Yet when this alchemy creates explosions
I wonder if you hear me when I praise.

CLYDE HURLSTON

BAPTIZED IN BLUE

After you kissed me with those perfect lips,
the rest of the world was always lost to me.
Do you remember how I would stare into your eyes,
in an effort to find my bearings again, darling?
That was because every single time
I shared the same space with you,
it made me feel like gravity no longer applied to me.
Your love just does something to me;
I struggle to find the words.
When you would look at me,
and baptize me in those loving blue eyes,
you made my soul feel reborn.
When you smiled at me,
I longed to learn the ways
I could somehow become a better man.
And when you'd say my name,
I swear I felt like God during morning mass.
How do you do these things you do, my love?
And won't you return, to finally do them again?

THAT'S WHAT SHE SAID

It's been said that time is unkind to memories.
And while i know this to be true,
the frequency with which mine are recalled,
has proven to do nothing but sharpen them.
With crystal clarity,
I remember the smile
that poured across her lips,
just before she kissed me.
And I recall her look of surprise,
as my hands grabbed her ass —
and proceeded to lift her off the ground.
And as long as I live,
I will never forget what she said
as she wrapped her legs around me.
Her soft hands touched my large face,
and she whispered,
"Mmm, that'll do it, baby.'

CLYDE HURLSTON

BEAUTY & THE BEAST

She looked up at me,
her eyes heavy
as if she had reached her wit's end.
And she said something to me
that I would not soon forget:
"Baby, I love that you're such a gentle
and respectful man with me.
It makes me feel loved.
It makes me feel safe.
But right now, I don't need that.
What I need is for you to take me
with those large arms of yours
and pin me down to this bed.
I need you to fuck me
like you have never loved me in your life.
And then when you're done with me,
and only then,
do I want you to hold me like you never stopped.
You've brought so much beauty into my life.
but after the day I've had, I need your beast."
And as I lifted her off the ground,
while walking intently to our bed,
I felt her let go of everything
that was weighing her down.
I knew then that she was completely mine...

A GRACE LIKE BRAILLE

Paradise has indeed been discovered,
But, it has sadly gone uncharted.
And oh, how i've longed to be the one
to remedy such an egregious oversight...
And finally, the goddess has acquiesced.
Her temple was then set to rest
upon an altar made of satin.
Her eyes, blindfolded for ceremony.
My hands, though rough from labor,
were soft with intention.
I exhaled nervously,
as my hands began to read
her grace like it was written in Braille.

CLYDE HURLSTON

WITH HANDS LIKE SEASONS

I've imagined us together a million times.
And in every dream,
you are the most beautiful thing I have ever seen.
And in those scenes, I come to you
with hands like the seasons.
Once I was winter.
Bitter. Stinging. Cold to the touch.
And then you kissed me...
Putting the spring in my wrist.
Writing feverishly.
Telling the world of the depths of your grace.
In the next dream, I leaned in to kiss you.
My large hand slid down
And brought summer between your legs.
I see you bite your lip,
hoping to stop yourself from letting go.
But it's too late... We both fall.
Into a lust that feels like love..
Time stops for you,
when my hand moves clockwise.
And your legs squeeze to hold it in place.
Darling, there is nothing more addictive
than the sounds you make,
with that look upon your face.

AGAIN, FOR THE LOTUS...

I've often wondered how you do it.
How can you mesmerize me
so effortlessly, my dear?
I have had to watch from afar as you fell apart,
time and time again.
Only to pick up the pieces
and put yourself back together.
Using just a touch of concealer to hide the scars,
and flashing a smile given by the gods
to distract your demons;
I've witnessed you strut your stuff in the mirror
as if you've never truly been hurt.
And I've read your words upon the page
and feared that you've never truly been loved.
Is it any wonder why I've called you my Lotus?
How you have resided within the mire
of the darkest nights,
and still greeted the sun each morning
more beautiful than you were the day before,
is beyond my understanding.
I swear I'm in awe of you.
Yet, like every work of art,
I must appreciate you from a distance;
much to my chagrin.
Still, there's not a soul on this Earth,
who can tell me that we're not lucky
to have seen you with our own eyes.
It is my hope, that you know this to be true;
and that one day, you'll believe it too.
Oh, how I wish it.

KINTSUGI

I have often seen you write of your brokenness.
Though your words were not in Braille,
I felt them all the same.
Your eloquence in describing the torture of a soul,
sends this supposed poet reeling.
For each time you do,
I realize that it is my tears that I am feeling
upon my face and not your own.
And as I struggle to regain my composure,
I catch myself wishing
that you could see yourself through my eyes.
Because if you did, you would see that you are
not a broken piece of pottery, darling.
Rather, you are a work of art;
reborn through Kintsugi.
It is then that I imagine my fingers
tracing the scars that I fear
once caused you shame.
And as my skin softly scoured
these proofs of your survival,
I would imagine each of them
had been filled with gold.
There would be no need for you to spill tears
in an attempt to water the garden
you have been told was barren.
There would be a time when you could rest,
and take refuge from the unseen war
you have had to endure within your temple.
You could simply be what the gods
intended you to be... Free.
And as you laid bare before me,
I would whisper in your ear and remind you
of the divinity you had possessed but forgotten.

THE SACRED GIFT OF FIRE

And then you would look up at me
with those eyes, my God those eyes…
just before we'd kiss
and discover new worlds together.

CLYDE HURLSTON

THE CRIES OF THE BEAST

In the dungeons of my soul,
there lies a direwolf.
Seemingly chained in place,
unable to do much
but pace about and wait.
Its thirst and its hunger
are oftentimes unbearable.
So out of rage and even desperation,
it begins to howl.
Calling out to a moon that it has never seen,
whose light it has never bathed beneath.
And not surprisingly,
those soul-wrenching howls
made their way throughout my veins,
and began to put this
all too familiar motion inside my wrist.
And that is why she came.
Unlike most,
she was able to read upon the page,
the cries of the beast
none have ever witnessed themselves.
She heard that which was
never carried upon a breath.
And in her wisdom,
she knew that without access to the wild,
the beast was only courting death.
And so she sought to free the wolf within the man!
She did this not out of pity,
and not in search of accolades;
but she did so out of love.
For she wanted to see him free...
Though in the back of her mind she knew,
it was her that he would devour!
Over and over again.
And between us, she was aching for it.

A WALKING DRUG

Everyone has an addiction.
Some can be purchased, others are given freely.
And while I can relate to the former,
I'm truly at the mercy of the latter.
My drug comes to me walking upright,
in stiletto heels no less.
A form most glorious.
My addiction knows I'm helpless.
A glance away from relapse.
One taste and what was once
a decoration in my veins, became a fixture.
She has dug in deep.
And she has no intentions of letting go.
And friend,
I don't mean to make addiction sound trivial,
but how else can I word this?
A want? A need?
An all-consuming craving?
Yeah, that'll do it.
As long as you have an idea
of how deep this desire goes.
From the subtle grays in my hair,
down to the bottoms of my toes.
Lightning in a bottle.
That's how her fingertips
cause such a stir in me.
You can have your diamonds
and expensive shoes.
You can keep your flatscreens, sports cars,
and rooms with breathtaking views.
I just need her. Over and over again.
And like the rest of those things,
if I work hard enough, we will all come in time.

CLYDE HURLSTON

MY NATIVE TONGUE

Her love was a language
In which my tongue
Once ached to gain fluency.
All of these years later,
Not only can I still remember
Just the way she likes it,
But on nights like this,
I can still taste the way
Her lessons came.

LA DANSE DANS LA VALLÉE

Her legs went up into the air like mountains;
As her elbows held her up, in a position just the same.
It has been a long time, since she's felt this alive.
The days bore down upon her with such a weight,
That even the nights brought her pain.
But right now, in this second, she was free.
As she collapsed backward onto the bed,
Her hands found their way into my hair;
As if to hold me in place as I drank from her chalice.
The legs that once made Kilimanjaro blush,
Now fashion themselves into a vise around my neck.
She feels so much closer to transcendence now;
And so I press forward with zeal.
I continue speaking in silent tongues,
The language that only she can understand.
And as her body quakes,
I know for a moment that her pain is gone.
So I proudly continue, allowing each lash of this tongue,
To course through her body like lightning.
And each time she trembles,
I can't help but to gaze upon my works.
I feel divine, as I hear my name decorate each space between her breaths.
For I am honored to be her medicine.

CLYDE HURLSTON

TO CATCH FIRE

For we few the others
have deemed skilled with the pen,
it is nothing to speak of desire.
Because we all know
what it feels like to burn for another;
but have we ever stopped and pondered
that moment in which we catch fire?
For me, it always starts in My Imagined Nation.
Just imagining having her all to myself.
To caress her skin.
Allowing my fingers to be baptized
in its softness and warmth.
Knowing the goosebumps my touch produced,
could be read like Braille.
As if her heart left a discrete message,
telling me to do anything but stop.
Then I allow myself to enjoy the smell of her.
Whether it's perfume or lotion,
it truly does not matter.
She wouldn't smell like anything around me.
And so I become lost;
and the desire to hold her overwhelms.
Then I notice her lips.
Are they full, are they thin?
What would they feel like?
What would they taste like?
How would they look
when my name escapes their grasp?
Then I imagine the kiss.
Starting softy and increasing with intensity.
My left hand, softly touching her face.
My right hand, embedded in her hair.
Then I imagine her hands.

THE SACRED GIFT OF FIRE

The kiss beginning to warm her in places
she can't quite reach.
So her soft hands begin exploring me.
Looking for exactly what she needs in that moment,
and being delighted as it rises up to greet her.

CLYDE HURLSTON

KISS THE SHORE

Tell me, have you ever sat in silence
And watched the ocean kiss the shore?
Have you witnessed the tides withdraw
Until the land finally begs for more?
Tell me, does this natural occurrence
Seem to mirror how our love
Was filled with legendary ebbs and flows
That we could never rise above?
Now I watch the power in these waves
And my mind recalls a scene with haste
It was the final time that we made love
And I gave your love a final taste.
Had I known there would never be
Another chance for me to drink
I would not have stopped until my tongue
Drove your mind right up to the brink
For past the edge of all sanity
Lies the kind of love I felt for you
But like those castles made of sand
We weren't meant to know if forever could be true.

GOOD MORNING, DARLING

I have often imagined waking up,
and rejoicing that you were in my bed.
I would simply lie there in awe,
as you slept so soundly;
wearing nothing but my t-shirt.
And as one of your legs
made its way from under the covers,
I would witness the morning sun
pour through my window
and make its way across your skin.
I couldn't help but to take my fingers
and trace the path the sun took.
Knowing full well that doing so,
would take my breath away.
And that's when I couldn't stand it any longer.
I would remove your covers with impatience.
I would simultaneously raise the cloth
that sought to hide your temple,
and I would part the gates outside of paradise.
As I began kissing the inside of your thighs,
I felt you start to stir.
But it wasn't until my tongue disappeared,
that you finally awoke.
And as I felt your hands
making their way into my hair,
I knew you didn't mind
becoming my breakfast in bed.
For I heard every single word,
that you never said.
As you neared the summit,
the arch in your back
could surely inspire the gods to praise themselves.
Still, I made no apologies

CLYDE HURLSTON

for continuing to have my way with you.
For you cause a hunger in me that cannot be sated.
That is why my fingers and tongue
conspired to make you cum,
long before "good morning, darling"
ever left your perfect lips.

BOOKMARK

Although
I didn't know her story,
Lord knows,
I longed to hold a page.

CLYDE HURLSTON

THE SWEET SONG OF SUNLIGHT

I have a feeling sunlight's better,
when it's tasted off your lips.
And I've watched as clouds would darken,
jealous of your fingertips.
I've heard as birds would sing us,
the sweetest of their songs.
And inside your eyes I'm finding,
the rights to all my wrongs.
But you don't seem to notice,
what's right in front of your eyes.
And most don't miss the sunlight,
'til clouds overtake the skies.
Some lie awake and wonder,
if the night is all they'll know.
But the sun returns with morning
to bathe us in its glow.

THE FINGERS OF A WRITER

Today I was reminded just how long it has been
since I was the focus of a woman's passion.
Like a single structure in the path
of an uncontrollable storm.
And while it was admittedly
not my proudest realization,
it was indeed an honest one.
After I suppressed that slight tinge of shame,
my mind recalled the fact
that the French sometimes refer to the orgasm
as la petit mort, "the little death."
And it inspired me to recall the myriad of times
I felt the most alive just before I died.
Naturally, this leads to thoughts of you, darling.
For instance,
I think of the last time we were together.
When I eagerly tasted
the desire pouring off of your lips,
as my hands began to explore the body
you entrusted to me on that night.
I watched as you began to move with closed eyes,
as if you were slowly attempting
to direct my large hand
exactly where you wanted it to go.
Only to watch you seconds later,
bite your lip in frustration,
as you realized exactly
who was in control of this particular journey.
I remember hearing the breath
escape your perfect lips,
as the hand that once wrote of you with pride,
began to deliver pleasure
by simply moving in a clockwise fashion.

CLYDE HURLSTON

Then I watched as pleasure turned to ecstasy
with the disappearance of a few well-placed fingers.
For it was my duty to warm
what would become my final resting place that night.
More than my pride began to swell,
as I noticed your garden
eagerly responded to its welcomed guests.
And as your temple grew more and more tense,
I could surmise
you were nearing the summit already,
and so the aforementioned guests
continued deeper and deeper into Eden,
until you sang your breathless song
as you finally let go of this world.
You were always such a sight to behold, baby.
Especially as you then tasted yourself
upon the fingers of this writer.

CLOCKWISE

I wonder if I bought you flowers,
would you just sit and let them wilt?
What if I impaled you with my love,
would you take it right up to the hilt?
Or would you point to circumstance,
and lay the blame upon its feet?
Could I gently slide my fingers in,
and turn your bitter into sweet?
Tell me all the things that trouble you,
as my hand goes clockwise for a time.
Lose yourself inside my words,
and bathe your subconscious in my rhyme.
Bring forth the ocean springs,
that could cleanse your worried heart.
For I want to see you come undone,
and I don't mean to fall apart.

CLYDE HURLSTON

GRAVITY

I'll never forget the heights we reached
For you once made this heavy man feel weightless.
Through the grace of your fingertips,
I was the bane of afternoon clouds.
And through the taste of your lips,
I was the envy of man-made rocket ships.
Do you remember how I once claimed to be
The reason there were footprints on the moon?
That was all because of you, darling.
Now, though I am reticent to admit this,
I am hoping another will come along
To eclipse what you did to me.
Because even though I've stopped
Holding my breath for your return,
I still miss having my breath taken away.
And I long to once again
Venture past the reaches of gravity.

THE SACRED GIFT OF FIRE

FIRESTARTER

For her, turning me on was effortless.
Just a look became a spark
A touch? That became a flame.
A kiss? That produced the fire.
And when I was granted entry inside of her,
The smoke would choke the gods.
For our efforts often singed the Garden.
Making those lucky enough to reside in Eden,
sweat like they were in Hell.

CLYDE HURLSTON

MY FAVORITE OF ALL

I've witnessed firsthand
the amazing things you can do
with your mouth, darling.
My favorite of all
was when your lips world slowly part,
so you could remind me
that you loved me.

COUNTING STARS

The only thing
I miss more than loving you,
Is the way my tongue
Would make you lose count
Of every single time
I took you to the stars
Without saying a word.

CLYDE HURLSTON

THE POWER THAT SHE WIELDS

Some days, I feel as if
I am a broken record of sorts.
For this pen,
often moves in a similar fashion.
It eagerly helps me to tell the world
the tallest tales of her.
All of which, I know to be true.
And all of which,
she is far too modest to say herself.
But deep down, in the places
my love has been known to reach,
she knows exactly
what she does to me.
I only bother to write it down,
so that the world may know
the power that she wields.
And also, to tell them of
the lucky man I've been.
Having tasted the divine in the flesh.

JUSTIFY THE WAIT

Photographs no longer do you justice,
And phone calls only make it worse.
It's hard for me to sleep at night,
When these visions won't disperse..
So it's then that the doors are locked,
And the sacred rituals performed.
The release arrives in waves,
Each helping to calm the storm.
But with the passing of some time,
The fires rise again.
Leaving smoke to fill the room,
And you're not here to breathe it in.
Which makes the animal in me,
Put stress upon restraints.
Causing these howls to be written down.
In place of just complaints.
Yet they somehow reach your ears,
And so your pulse begins to race.
Because your desires mirror mine,
Having long been denied a taste.
So now this bed must become the cross,
On which we will sacrifice.
The hours we have spent apart,
Knowing the growth from distance won't suffice.
So my darling, won't you please return,
Before it's far too late?
Then I'll watch you resurrect this part of me,
With lips that always justify the wait.

LOVE-STARVED (PART 1 OF 2)

When it came to you darling,
There was a time when I wore my hunger
Like a badge of honor.
Humility often gave way to hubris,
As I allowed my hands to strut across this page,
And tell the world how I longed for you.
Believing that no other man
Could love you the way that I did,
I thought that by displaying
the depths of this ache
I could bring you back to me.
As it turns out,
I was nothing more than a love-starved fool.
Mistaking his hunger pains
as cosmic signs from the gods.
Urging me to continue on;
As if groveling would win the day.
Not realizing that I was instead repelling,
The very thing I wished to keep.
But when you've been alone for most of your life,
You are often unaware
Of just how ugly desperation can be.
And how close unrequited love
Can feel like famine.

BINGE LOVER (PART 2 OF 2)

Just one taste of you was not enough, darling;
I needed more.
For your love was
the greatest thing I have ever tasted.
And after being forced to fast for so long,
I was hellbent on making up for lost time.
I was on a binge for your love;
And there wasn't an ounce
of goddamn shame that I felt.
I remember you felt the same way then.
We moved Heaven and Earth to get together
Twice in just those few days.
You knew how Famished I was
From the first kiss I placed below your waist.
And that first second I was inside of you,
You may as well have been in my veins;
because I was gone..
On a natural high of euphoria and lust.
Thanks to you, passion had become
The last meal of a dying man;
And it brought him back to life.
Little did I know,
that I would spend the next few years
Chasing the taste
of that which I never got to own.

CLYDE HURLSTON

IN A STATE OF RITUAL

Lying here on a Sunday morning,
My thoughts are bathed in sin.
Visions replaying in my head,
Have left me in this state again.
I take the quickest look around,
And find the monument is raised.
But she is not beside me so,
It's a sight that's lacking praise.
But still, the potent urge is there,
To help it see the light of day.
And perform the sacred ritual,
That will help it go away.
So I guess I'll have to close my eyes,
And proceed without an ounce of shame.
Until the gods are satisfied,
I perform the act whilst calling out her name.

THE HANDS OF THE UNDESERVING

I'm sure I sound
like a broken record by now, friend...
But would you like to know
The worst part of being without her?
It's knowing that a woman like her actually exists,
And I'll never again be able to call her my own.
For she now lies in the hands of the undeserving;
And there's nothing I can do about it.
Even as they ignore the way
she hides behind her hand,
When she's trying not to laugh.
Or the way her eyes would sparkle,
When you took her photograph.
They'll never care to greet her with a whisper,
When her day was long.
Nor will they gaze at her in awe,
And wonder how she got to be so strong.
They'll never kiss her gently
The way a woman should be kissed.
And they'll never kiss her harder,
To show her that she was missed.
And he will never take the time,
To learn the difference between her sighs.
Since he only wants to keep her happy,
So he can get between her thighs.
And it's not to say that I'm a saint,
Or that she's with the devil now in hell.
But when a man really loves a woman,
It's not hard for you to tell.
And though I'm so very far from perfect,
I can say this without hyperbole.
There's not a man upon this Earth,
That would've loved her more than me.

CLYDE HURLSTON

A SCULPTOR'S PLEA

Oh, how unfair it is...
You know exactly the effect you have on me.
And still you tease me like you do.
Knowing damn well.
That I long for those moments
I can make you mine.
When my fingers can trace
every inch of your skin.
As if it were a map leading me to a treasure,
I have never seen before.
But the truth is, I have seen it.
I've imagined us together so many times,
That you'd think these hands
sculpted you from my dreams.
Yet here you are, alive to fascinate me.
And distant enough to torture me.
Oh, darling, put me out of my misery:
Let me have a taste of you.

NO SUBSTITUTES

In the past, you made me chase;
and I did so like a fool.
But now I feel I must remind you,
my world is under a new rule.
For the old me would've held his breath,
and endured your every tease.
Instead the new king throws a pillow on the floor,
to protect your willing knees.
Yes, in the past, the old me would've caved
whilst not expressing my demands.
But now I tell you to open up your mouth,
as I take your hair inside my hands.
Because I love that talking back,
is not all your mouth can do.
And so my hands guide your pretty face,
until I decide that you are through.
But then you increase your speed,
trying to see my knees get weak.
So the King becomes the Beast,
who will growl instead of speak.
And by holding you in place,
your perfect eyes well up with tears.
Darling. I marvel at your skill,
as my monument disappears.
And the motion in your hands,
makes the clouds begin to swell.
While the smile upon your face,
lets me know that you can tell.
That is when your lips and hands conspired,
to make your fabled King explode.
And it's with my every ounce of love,
that I give every drop you're owed.
Because when you're the best at what you do,

CLYDE HURLSTON

you're sure to find your way into my rhyme.
And that is why I accept no substitutes,
until I can once again make you mine.

INTOXICATED

Often I've wondered,
how can she be so effortlessly fascinating?
How can she be so far away, and still
mesmerize me in the way that she does?
Yet, when asked, she swears
that she's not doing anything;
but her smile proves that deep down,
we both know that is a lie.
For the love of perseverance,
how am I supposed to resist such a force?
Intoxicated, I hang on every letter of her every word.
Like a true lush, she leaves me stumbling
and hanging on to this metaphoric flask for dear life.
Just for another sip of her.
Still, every conversation feels like
I'm tugging at the bow atop a gift
that no one can see but me.
And it's in these moments,
that I beg the gods for forgiveness;
because selfishness has gotten the best of me again.
And I dream of giving her every inch of the rest of me...
if only she so desired.
Does this smile on my face make me suicidal?
Or am I simply a glutton for the one
who makes me feel hunger in my bones?
I can't tell the difference anymore.

CLYDE HURLSTON

THE MAGIC YOU PRACTICE

What is this power you have over me?
How have you invaded
even my waking thoughts?
How is it that you are able to dance
around the bonfires in my mind,
all the while, pretending not to notice me burning?
Do you not see what you do to me?
Is it your unspoken desire
to use that which you harden without effort
as but another piece upon the pyre?
Won't you help to make this reality manifest?
How many more Rituals Of Loneliness
must I fucking perform,
before you will part the sea between us,
and help me calm the storm?
Come now darling...
Let me experience
this magic that you practice.

THE SACRED GIFT OF FIRE

LONG FOR THE DAY

You've been gone for so long,
I honestly couldn't fault you
for thinking that I have forgotten.
But I haven't, love. I remember it all.
But I long for the day
when you begin to remember.
I know you did what you had to do.
Just to get through your days,
you had to bury what we had
far beneath what you've been settling for.
That way you would no longer feel it smolder;
you would no longer see the smoke.
And eventually, you forgot how it feels to burn.
But i bet if you looked
into these brown eyes of mine,
you'd remember, darling.
You'd recall with clarity,
the way you stirred the beast in me
with just a turn of phrase.
You would quickly recollect
how you could cause this monument to raise,
simply by holding my gaze.
You are my temptation made flesh, baby.
And by God, I long for the day
when you're once again ready to play.
And let me have my way with you.

CLYDE HURLSTON

ESOTERIC EROTICA

This type of potent chemistry
cannot be left to chance.
This type of union
bears only the fingerprints of the gods.
For who else but them
could produce such alchemy?
Tell me, who else but you,
could cause this Greek fire within me?
We both know the answer, darling.
So let us not pretend
ike we did not exhale each other's smoke
after each kiss, my love.
And let us not pretend that when my risen blade
was placed within your waiting chalice,
that the planets did not converge inside our eyes.
For I felt your spirit move each time
my love was taken to its base.
And my faith in life was renewed,
each time I saw that look upon your face.
That is why you should return to me:
No other man can fill you up
Until your very soul has runneth over.

A CURE FOR NUMBNESS

I know I sound like
A broken record at this point,
But I really needed to see you.
As much as I love talking to you online,
Or even hearing your voice on the phone,
There is absolutely no substitute
For seeing your face with my own eyes.
There is no replacing the feeling I have
As your skin touches mine.
The heat we produce is unmistakable.
And it is that very heat,
Which thaws my heart and soul.
Allowing me to feel again
And as your hands touch my face,
The numbness dissipates
As you draw closer.
And as we kiss
For the first time in years,
I am alive again.

SILENT HYMNS

It has been longer than
I would care to admit, darling;
Still, this extended duration
Has done nothing to temper
The zeal with which
I always wish to proceed.
You wouldn't know it
from my actions, though.
Because I know how much
You love a slow hand
In certain places.
But at the end of the day,
I can only sate my hunger for so long.
Eventually,
I am going to need to taste you
Until you say you love me.
Just as I have in every life
That we have ever lived.
For while I may be out of practice,
I haven't forgotten the silent hymns
That made you call out for the Lord.

INTERNAL STORMS

Darling,
There is a storm brewing inside of me.
I can hear the thunder growling
Deep within this darkness of mine.
The temperatures have fallen steadily
And you are no closer
To resuming your place beside me.
Are you really so bold as to forsake
The consequence of nature?
For I know damn well,
That because of the lackluster
Quality of explorers in the world,
Your valleys have long since run dry.
And your peaks have not been reached
Since we last saw each other.
Yet here you are,
Letting time get in the way of destiny.
Allowing circumstances to once again
Place excuses upon your perfect tongue
Instead of the tip of my love.
How dare you give me hope,
And then once again
Start seeking shelter elsewhere.
When it is clear
That my love was made to rain,
Only upon your plains.

DRY-MOUTHED

I must admit, darling,
It is getting harder to remember
The last time I was allowed
To have a taste of Eden.
But on nights like this,
All I have to do is concentrate
And the images flood my mind.
Memories are no comparison
To the real thing, mind you;
But with such a distance between us,
They will have to suffice for now.
Still, I cannot help but feel dry-mouthed
When I think about how long it's been
Since I've had a drink of you.
I can still recall the way
Your fingers cascade through my hair
As my tongue began reciting
Its SIlent Hymns inside
The only temple it considers to be holy.
And I forget just how strong you are
Until your hands and thighs
Trap and keep me exactly where you need
My tongue to continue mining.
I wonder if this is how Jacob felt
When he wrestled his angel that day.
But, if breath must be sacrificed
So that you may reach release,
I was always more than willing
To suffocate for you, my love.
In fact, I am dying to do so again.
Whenever you are ready.

BREATHLESS CONFIRMATIONS

There wasn't a place on her supple body,
That I didn't explore.
Each new place I softly touched,
Became yet another reason
For her to gasp slightly
And exhale her
Breathless confirmations.
I eagerly continued searching
For ways to get her past
The point of no return.
And I am honored
That she let me claim
Every inch of her,
In the name of love.

CLYDE HURLSTON

MAGNUM OPUS

I can only say this but so many ways, my love.
These lines are to be a mere substitute
until we are reunited.
For I know many will peruse these lines
and seek to read between them,
but I can only think of licking my fingers
before turning the pages
you have kept from me for too long.
And while these metaphors
may run too deep for some,
you've always made the room to handle them.
And that is why only you
can feel the full extent of the power in this quill.
Only the sacred touch of your hands and your lips
could put the motion in this wrist.
And only your garden can make this love grow
past the point of longing.
But the gods know,
how you love to make me wait for it.
So that is why, the next time I see you,
I plan on giving you my magnum opus.
With the depths this poem will reach inside of you,
you'll be feeling it for days afterward, darling.
I fucking swear it.

WELL-PLACED HANDS

With her, everything was different.
Hell, I can even say,
That I was different with her.
You see, for most of my life,
I have been timid.
I am a very large man, dear reader;
So I must be careful at all times.
Every thought and every action
Must be controlled.
For I do not want
To cause harm for others.
I have never wanted to be feared
By those I truly loved.
Yet, she could sense what hid within me.
She could tell
There was a beast inside of me
That was dying to get out.
So she made it her mission to wake it.
With her well-placed hands,
And her ever-perfect lips
Reciting the magic words,
She willingly and eagerly became the place
Where it was safe for me to let go.
Where I was free to lose control,
And have my fucking way with her.

CLYDE HURLSTON

THE POTENCY OF POETRY

In the past, I often wished
for you to get drunk upon these words of mine.
As if my every line were wine,
or if each word I happened to jot,
would warm you inside like another shot.
I wanted your perfect lips to know only my taste.
And that's not to say
you couldn't sample the work of others, mind you.
I would never seek to control
your every move or thought.
I just wanted you to know
that when the time came for you to get a buzz,
where the home of the strongest proof was.
And that would always be here with me.
Whether my words were spoken or written,
they should always be taken straight with no chaser.
And thankfully, you were skilled enough
to handle it by the page, weren't you, darling?
My only regret is that my words
were the only thing of mine
you ever allowed inside of you.
If given the chance,
the potency of my poetry
wouldn't have been the only reason
you were stumbling drunk, baby.
Because if you think
these words of mine are something serious,
you should have taken a ride upon my love.
Then you would have discovered that
the quill reaches far deeper than the ink,
when it is made to be stiffer than your favorite drink.

WATCH ME WRITE

She said she wanted to watch me write,
but I rarely did it upon command.
Because I needed inspiration,
before there was movement in my hand.
To which she would inquire,
if I had found myself a muse.
As if there were a waiting wick,
that required a spark to light its fuse.
So I responded with the truth,
and started telling her about.
How my last had left a burning fire,
And never stopped to put it out.
But since it lacked a constant source of fuel,
the fire failed to grow.
Leaving only ash behind,
here upon the page to show.
The remnants of a love,
that not many would ever feel.
And because she could see my scars,
she knew I was for real.
That's when concern ensnared her voice,
and she asked to see my quill.
Saying someone with my kind of skills,
shouldn't lack a place to fill.
So she took it upon herself,
to breathe life into my pen.
And as I held her hair in place,
the ink began to flow again.
But after many minutes passed,
I neared the end of this metaphoric road.
So I had to make it clear to her,
this quill wanted to explode.
Still, she continued on,

CLYDE HURLSTON

without an ounce of fear.
And that's when the ink began to spill,
yet this story, I will end it here.

INTERNAL REMINDERS

If you only knew,
how it pains me to know you, darling.
Don't get me wrong, your friendship
has been nothing short of a blessing to me.
And I shall do my very best not to lose it.
Having said that,
nothing makes this pain of mine subside.
On cold nights like this,
I want to be the reason
you are warm in places you cannot reach.
On cold nights like this, I ache to be the reason
You lose hours of sleep,
only to be worn out and exhausted the next day.
And on cold nights like this, I wouldn't rest
until you felt the love I had for you so deeply,
your insides were sore.
As you walked out the door in the morning,
you would still feel where I'd been, baby.
You would be left wet
from internal reminders of what it means
to have your needs met.
I would take care of you in a fashion
that would please the gods and
awakened souls alike.
But alas, it is not to be.
For you don't see me that way;
and until now, I could understand why.
Still, I can't help but wonder
what fires we could have made,
on cold nights like this.

CLYDE HURLSTON

MIRACLE WORKER

I had known quite a few women
that would talk a big game, darling.
Just as I'm sure you had been sold
a bill of goods by many dishonest men.
Yet, I knew something about you
was different from the rest.
Whether it was the benefit of instinct,
or loneliness whispering in my ears,
I truly didn't care at that point.
No, by then, I simply wanted
to learn every single thing
that your perfect mouth could do.
And so, I watched in wonder...
As you combined breath and spit,
to make that which had no bone,
hard enough to break.
And with my hands full of your hair,
you showed me
how much of it you could take.
It was then I knew:
I was finally witnessing
a true miracle worker.

RECIPE FOR GROWTH

The look in her eyes
always takes me to another place.
When she's ready to go like this,
I need to make sure
not a second goes to waste.
For when the fire has been set,
patience is no longer one of her virtues.
No, only vices will reign tonight.
And it seems I can't get my jeans off fast enough.
Thankfully, they're not very tight.
She's been tearing at my belt
since my body touched the bed.
In fact, I can't even remember
the last thing that she said.
I just the love the way she moves with purpose;
never leaving room for doubt to join us.
With my hands in her hair now,
I never have to abandon hope.
And when she takes me in her mouth,
breath and spit will make
the perfect recipe for growth.
And once she gets her rhythm,
she makes it difficult to think.
I feel her nose touch my navel,
her only reflex is to wink.
By the gods, she's the best at this,
I shouldn't have to say it twice.
And as she aims to suck my stress away,
I am a willing sacrifice.
But then I thrust my love into her mouth,
when I feel I'm getting close.
It seems she wants her medicine,
and I'm inclined to share a dose.

CLYDE HURLSTON

My muscles begin to tighten,
as I feel each wave of my release.
Her hands and mouth are united,
and their movements never cease.
Now you see why I've been wrapped around her finger,
the way she always has to have my sword.
And you'd confuse me for a religious man,
the way she makes me praise the Lord.

THE SEA OF SHEETS

Like stray cats in the night,
moonlight plays upon the street.
And it's then I often think of her,
and wonder if she thinks of me.
As my heart begins to roar,
like drums that call for war.
Does she picture all her clothes,
in a pile upon my floor?
Because I've not perfected love,
but for her I'd surely try.
As I long for my hands to be the ones,
that helped her inhibitions die.
I picture her legs around my neck,
as they flow like waves upon my back.
As she arches off the bed,
with a grace she thought she lacked.
I hear her pray in whispers,
each one ending with my name.
As we were lost inside the sea of sheets,
that my tired bed became.
And then her muscles tightened,
crying out for sweet release.
Her hands would find my hair,
to ensure she'd reach her peace.
But as she started shaking,
and collapsed upon the bed.
I understood every single word,
my goddess never said.

CLYDE HURLSTON

THE FIRST PILLAR: SELF-DISCOVERY

I often wonder if you know
just how many nights
that I imagine you, darling.
Barely-dressed,
yet safely tucked in your bed at home.
The latest volume of my work in one hand,
a glass of wine in the other.
Your intoxicating eyes
pouring over my words in earnest;
whilst the rest of you
is simultaneously aching to see
if you will find yourself between the lines.
I then imagine the whispered gasp
that leaves your lips,
once you decode the phrases
meant for you and you alone.
And so in a rush of joy mixed with adrenaline,
your hand finds its way between your legs;
tracing the perfect path
to another session of self-discovery.
For no one knows your combination
better than you do, my love.
And there has never been a thing I have wanted
unlocked more than your temple.
So I imagine your fingers going with
and then against the grain,
as if the clock beside you holds no sway.
Oh, how I've prayed to own the name you'd say,
as you began coming undone.

THE SECOND PILLAR: THE GROWTH

And after you have measured your reading,
and truly found yourself wanting,
there is no turning back for you.
There can only be one ending to this night,
if both of our sanities are to remain intact:
we must devour each other!
And so the overdue nature of my arrival
is outweighed only by your aggressive impatience.
My shirt finds the floor,
mere seconds after the closing of the door.
Your hands are at my belt,
and there isn't any time left for greetings or inquiries.
With haste, my pants too
become another victim of the times.
Your eyes light up as I stand before you,
in the same glory you have shown to me.
Your hands find their highly-favored place,
and I watch you prepare your lips without a word.
You always enjoy this part: the growth.
A sharp inhale of breath,
and you eagerly baptize my love
in the warmth of your mouth.
I feel your fingernails exploring my legs,
as this part of me swells and gets larger
through the work of your tongue.
You love having this power over me, don't you?
You needn't say it,
for the speed of your nods tells me so.
Oh, fuck they tell me, darling.
So don't stop.
Now with two handfuls of your hair,
I aim to aid a master who needs no assistance.
And so, I just watch you work.

CLYDE HURLSTON

THE THIRD PILLAR: THE TASTE

Impatient as ever, you're now lying on the bed,
waiting for me to journey past the gates.
To reunite the blade with its chalice,
and resume our sacred union.
But not just yet, my love.
Before I can make
my grand entrance into the temple,
the arrival must be preceded by the taste.
Feeling my lips kissing their way up your thighs,
and feeling my warm breath near your garden
finally calms you down.
I know you've seemingly been waiting forever, baby.
But it pales in comparison
to the eons I've spent searching for you.
So now that we're here, my hunger must be sated.
And tonight, you are the only thing I wish to eat.
So I watch as you lay your head back,
and drape a leg on each of my shoulders.
You are safe now.
So now it is I that draws a sharp breath,
and begins to drink.
With each rise and fall of my tongue,
I feel your body mirror its movements.
With such grace and fluidity,
you are the envy of the oceans.
And as my second finger follows the first to explore,
it is clear from your sound,
and your arching body that you are wanting more.
So I slowly increase my speed.
The pressure on my ears
from your vise-like thighs,
tells me that we are nearing your altitude, darling.
I must press onward
until you've collapsed and fight to catch your breath.
Now I feel the beast in me awaken...

THE FOURTH PILLAR: CONTROL

Darling, by now you should know
that the hands of control
don't always belong to tyrants.
No, sometimes they belong to lovers
who have been made to wait too long.
And by the time fortune favors their undertaking,
wants have grown like weeds;
unintentionally turning into needs.
So it is then, I bend you over this bed.
The first entrance is taken all the way to the base.
You close your eyes as tightly
as you surround my love.
But as my left hand takes a handful of your hair,
You know exactly what fate awaits you.
As my right hand
leaves its large prints across your ass,
you'd swear I was finger painting for the gods.
But as that same hand
squeezes down upon your hip,
it is obvious that on some nights
a lack of mercy isn't necessarily cruel.
Because we both know this is what you wanted.
So tell me who the fuck it belongs to, baby.

CLYDE HURLSTON

THE FIFTH PILLAR: SURRENDER

When it comes to this form of art,
just as it is in all aspects of life,
there must be balance.
That is why as wildly
as I indulged in having control of you,
I must now be willing to lay down my arms,
and provide you with my surrender.
The sweat glistening off of our bodies,
aids in the changing of positions.
Now I witness your slight ascension,
as you bring yourself down upon my love.
All the way down, in a fashion that would inspire
a recital of Job 38:11; if only I could speak.
But I could only watch as you rose again.
Going up and down upon my hardened gift;
as if it were Jacob's Ladder.
I watched you place your hands atop my chest,
so you could focus on your form,
as you carried yourself to Heaven.
I swear the sounds you made
were so divine in tone,
they could make the angels weep.
Whilst they watched over us,
as we did everything but sleep.
Still, you rode me with such intensity,
I believed your demons
would never again catch up with you.
But I didn't know how much longer I could hold on,
before you made me explode.

THE SIXTH PILLAR: RELEASE

With each angle you took upon the Ladder,
I found it more and more difficult to adjust.
Still, I foolishly believed myself to be formidable
in the ways of pleasing you.
In truth, you are the gateway to the universe,
so I never stood a chance.
That didn't mean I would go down without a fight.
That is when I rolled over on top of you,
placing your legs atop my shoulders.
You were as fearless as you were helpless.
While I was as ravenous as I was merciless.
For once again,
I began to pound your shores like the tide.
I could not apologize
for the pain I caused you inside.
Because you knew,
we were both on a collision course with release.
So you simply dug your nails in,
and begged me not to cease.
It was then that harder and faster
became my unspoken hymn.
Your legs began to shake,
signaling you were ready for this to end.
And so I closed my eyes and raced
toward the final stretch.
Feeling every bit of your amazing grace,
squeeze around this hardened wretch.
It was then the dam gave way,
and my love began to pour.
A rebirth that felt like dying,
flooded us without an ark nor oar.
As I collapsed beside you on the bed,
you'd place your head upon my chest.

CLYDE HURLSTON

And the smile upon your face,
tells me that I have earned my rest.
...Oh, how I love you, darling.

END OF ACT 2

"I would put my lips to your canvas, taste where the sweat dripped from the paintbrush, and the thick, metallic earthiness of your skin.

I would run my tongue over the ridges of your beautifully crafted surface, kiss where the colors meet the edge of the frame. Claim it all as mine."

— Marisa Donnelly

"There wasn't an inch of her that he didn't taste; from the base of her throat to the curve of her waist to the backs of her knees to her candy apple-red toenails. And when he finally tasted the already damp petals of her womanhood, she tangled her fingers in his hair and arched her hips as the tremors of ecstasy shook her body. He felt each spasm as acutely as if she were connected to him."

- Bonnie Pega

ACT III
Explosions In The Temple

"The sexual embrace can only be compared with music and with prayer." - Marcus Aurelius

"To be intimate is to be in tune. Every corner of your body is an earthquake. That's how you make love to a woman." - Unknown.

CLYDE HURLSTON

"Exploration By The Inch" Art by Sir Render

UNDERGOING RENOVATIONS

You must be exhausted.
Because in my mind,
You have been mine several times.
Each time your temple was punished
In a fashion most proper.
You were stretched out and folded
In so many beautiful ways,
That origami would curse your name
out of jealousy.
And rest assured, darling,
You thoroughly enjoyed
the duration of your impalement.
Your eyes were closed so tightly,
I thought your mind was undergoing renovations.
Your skin was electric to the touch,
And your garden was generous with its juices;
Allowing me to make myself at home
Without any physical discomfort.
Unless you so desired it, of course.

CLYDE HURLSTON

ALCHEMY

Today, much like centuries past,
this practice was forbidden.
Often derided by the uninitiated as immoral,
and decried by the pious as the devil's work.
But all of them were wrong.
The spark is all that matters.
Transmutation breathes the air of divinity.
All other perspectives fall prey to semantics.
She was the only element I needed.
For it was at the very base of my being,
that I was broken.
Through her touch, I became whole.
In time, one could even say noble.
Her love made the impossible seem effortless.
Like turning lead into gold.
One look from her, and inside I am alive.
One kiss from her, and inside I am ablaze.
And at the first moment I'm inside of her, I am a god.
Through our union there is alchemy.
Nothing else makes life worth living.

THE SACRED GIFT OF FIRE

REMEMBER MY NAME

I don't know how else to say it,
but I've imagined it countless times.
Hidden it beneath the metaphors,
in all my countless rhymes.
I've imagined myself destroying you,
between your gasps and shortened breaths.
Your hands clinging tightly to the sheets,
as if to give them certain deaths.
Leaving you proudly at my mercy,
and like a god I impose my will.
Thinking of all of the lonely nights,
that I had too much time to kill.
So now you'll endure the punishment,
and find pleasure in the pain.
Knowing good and goddamn well,
you'll remember every letter of my name.
I implore you to survive the way I'll stretch,
and enjoy the way I'll fold.
Feel free to bite your lip,
as I take a handful of hair to hold.
And with every single thrust,
I use both love and hate as fuel.
With your heart I'm always gentle,
but tonight, to your garden I am cruel.
So I'll continue this destruction,
until you beg me not to stop.
And you'll serenade me with your moans,
until the last grain of sand decides to drop.

CLYDE HURLSTON

THE LOVER'S CRUCIFIX

Do you have any idea what it takes
to get through the day without you?
I don't believe you do, my love.
And yet it's the night
that always brings the pain of withdrawals.
It's getting much too hard for me to sleep.
And I don't mean difficult, love.
The visions are always the same.
You are lying down,
surrendered to me in trust.
And I am the animal inside you,
a truth reaffirmed with every thrust.
And while my hand moves with rhythm,
in the dream I lose control.
Trying to bury my love so deep inside,
you will feel it in your soul.
I hold down your extended hands,
as if you're crucified.
Tonight there's a rage within my lust,
that will not be denied.
So you wrap your legs around the god,
you've called out to with your breath.
As you sacrifice your cares,
and introduce your worries to their death.
You struggle to endure,
the depths that I explore.
But the ocean you release,
leaves me exploding like before.

SEISMIC ACTIVITY

Few things in this world
can make a man feel like a god.
And normally, humility won't let me say this,
but that night... I felt like a god inside of you.
In the moment, your eyes were so far away,
I could see constellations in them.
The deeper I went,
the more the Earth moved for you.
And you were the envy
of richter scales everywhere, darling.
At the epicenter of pleasure.
Oh, you were so alive when you came.
Each time, your inhibitions fell
like tired veils, until you lost count.
You were wild. Riding lightning in human form.
Our seismic activity was so profound.
Felt with magnitude by two.
And yet, I did not rain all over you.
but I will given the chance.
For that explosion is long overdue.

CLYDE HURLSTON

UNAPOLOGETIC GODS

I'm much too reserved in person.
So despite my stature,
you may not notice me.
But in my mind?
That kingdom behind my eyes?
You have been mine at least a thousand times.
I have left this chair,
like Zeus descending from Olympus;
and pinned you to the nearest wall,
as if you were fine art.
I have held handfuls of your hair,
the way Poseidon held his trident;
and ravaged you from behind.
I have lain you beneath me,
and pounded your shores like the tide.
Darling, I am gentle when you crave it.
But I am merciless,
when you have misbehaved.
And no one knows the lengths I would go,
to give you every inch of mine.
In my mind, we divide and conquer,
like unapologetic gods.
And oh, if you only knew
what I dreamed of doing to you,
during those times
that your beauty leaves me silent…

THE SACRED GIFT OF FIRE

FACEDOWN INTERROGATIONS

Do you find me sadistic, darling?
Because in truth, I'm not.
But you know that.
Since I was actually a masochist around you.
Waiting for you to stop forsaking me.
And maybe even notice the cross I carried for you.
Engraved proudly with your name..
But I've finally laid that burden down, dear.
Now I am in control.
And now, I've found myself a willing submissive.
Granted, she doesn't belong to me either.
But that doesn't make her any less beautiful
when she's looking up at me.
Or when she's laying on her back.
See? She isn't afraid like you were.
Her? She intentionally wakes the monster.
She does this knowing damn well
She will endure the punishment for your crimes.
Your neglect.
And her facedown interrogations last for hours.
I fold her every which way but free.
All because of things you never did for me.
And as her body rains,
She demands her sacrifice continue.
So I oblige.
Because I'm tired of waiting
for you to come to your senses.
So I make her cum instead.
And as her eyes roll into her head,
And she fights to find the breath to speak,
She sees the truth.
And she thanks you for being such a fucking fool.

FOG

She knows my combination well.
A few twists and turns, my inhibitions dissipate.
And I begin to come undone.
She has a subtle way of lighting this spark.
Two prolonged kisses,
and she stops midway through the third;
and then she just looks at me.
Making me feel like the luckiest man alive.
Then she flashes a sly and subtle smile,
before she leans in to finish what she started.
And just like that... I'm gone.
I never know where I go.
But it's goodbye, Dr. Jekyll;
and hello Mr. Clyde.
And I go from humble king
to raging beast in her hands.
I tear into her like I haven't eaten in years.
The arch in her back
is the envy of the crescent moon
that draws in the tides.
And I watch the oceans in her eyes widen,
as I enter her temple with reckless abandon.
I engage in the ancient arts of demolition
until the fog in my mind clears.
And finally, as we were adrift
in the seas of our own creation,
I remember exactly who I am.
And I know for sure,
I will never love another soul the way I love her.

THE MISSING PIECE

Tell me, darling...
The last time I was inside of you,
Did I reach the edges of your soul?
Did I then provide the missing piece,
That helped the puzzle become whole?
Was the way you shook another sign,
Was Heaven within your reach?
Or did the angels come crashing down
Fearing Eden had been breached?
Was the way you collapsed into my arms
Proof you saw the summit from your peak?
Was your descent without control?
Or did I leave you without a word to speak?
Darling, have you recovered from what we've done?
Or are you simply biding time?
Until my hand once again grips your throat
And the name you're screaming is mine.

CLYDE HURLSTON

YOUR BRAND OF PLEASURE

I honestly don't know if I can forgive you
for leaving me in this state, my love.
When you knew damn well,
that if I were to go this long
without your brand of pleasure,
it would only cause me pain.
Especially with each of us
knowing the other's combination so well...
But after all of this time, darling,
I think I know why you won't look me in the eyes.
It's because you don't want me to know
that you still ache for me in places you can't reach.
You haven't forgotten the way
your hands swam inside my hair,
the last time I got to taste you.
And you damn sure remember
how deep inside of you I once reached,
ever since you had to settle for a love
that barely skims the surface.
With him, you're not even happy to be here;
and with me, you lost count
of the times you came.
So why must you allow yourself
to merely be tolerated,
when you can recall a time
where you were once exalted?

MADE TO RAIN

Late at night, I must confess,
I often find myself wondering about you.
With nothing left to get me high
but the fumes of memories,
my mind begins to dredge up
the most beautiful images of you in my bed.
And it is then that I begin to think,
"When was the last time
you were made to rain, darling?
Has life had its way with you for so long,
that you've forgotten
what it's like to be at the mercy
of a man who loves you more than life?
Tell me, how long has it been
since your long legs adorned broad shoulders
in anticipation of what was next?
How long has it been since the arch in your back
was the envy of St. Louis,
as you were tasted like there was no tomorrow?
How long has it been
since your eyes rolled back into your head,
just a few seconds after penetration?
Tell me, how long has it been
since you were safe upon your back,
and your King was so deep inside you,
that he was reaching the edges of your soul?
I know how long it has been;
but I would rather not say.
For I know that your current situation
is anything but royal;
and since you urged me to move on,
I have been anything but loyal.
Yet we both know this choice was made for me,

CLYDE HURLSTON

though my hands are far from clean.
I guess, I have no other option but the next life,
unless my subconscious reunites us in a dream.
But tell me darling,
what good are those
when compared to the real thing?

WHISPERING TO THE GODS

I will never forget the gasp that escaped your lips,
the first time you slowly slid down
to the base of my love.
I marveled as you placed
your hands upon my chest,
so that you could raise and lower yourself at will;
with the intensity of your choosing.
Proudly impaling your garden
on this sword once fit for stone.
But oh, how your temple held it in place, my love.
As the divine tightness of your warmth
sought to bring out the beast in me,
you had no choice
but to be worn out from the inside.
I imagined the drops of sweat
upon your perfect breasts
became diamonds as my tongue
carried them away with haste.
I could taste the power in our efforts, darling.
I knew that with each adjustment,
every angle you tried,
I only reached further into your soul.
There was no stopping what was to come.
Every time your head titled back in ecstasy,
I could imagine the prayers
you were whispering to the gods
in between your moans;
had I not been busy doing the same.
As I pushed down on your hips,
and thrusted upward into Heaven,
I witnessed your legs begin to shake;
just as I could feel the pressure
building inside of my own love.

CLYDE HURLSTON

Unable to take anymore, I began to explode
just as you were reaching your own summit.
Breathless, you collapsed into my waiting arms.
Knowing you would find refuge between them.
There you stayed; and there we prayed..
To each other.

THIS FABLED SWORD

As the minutes bloom and become hours,
I watch as they wilt and give way to days.
I have lost count of them
since I've last seen your face;
and I'm not doing well with that, darling.
It seems that life's cruel circumstances
are once again conspiring to keep us apart.
And given the way the flames
dance when we are together,
one could hardly blame them;
since they are often forced to choke
on the billows we produce.
Still, I am here and I am waiting for you, baby;
rather impatiently, I might add.
For I need you to
quiet my demons with your touch.
Oh, how desperately
I need you to reawaken my soul with your kiss.
And if I'm being honest,
the time for you
to unsheathe this fabled sword is long overdue.
Because this most powerful weapon I wield
requires something essential to help it keep its edge.
It cries out for the whetstone
so well hidden within your temple.
That which sharpens and further hardens my love,
with each passing, passionate thrust.
How am I to maintain the level of skill you require,
without the one thing that makes me better?
And that is you, my love.
Know that these large arms are waiting to hold you
and to fold you when you are ready.
Once your storms finally pass,

CLYDE HURLSTON

and the waters are calm again,
you have but to say my name...
And I will be there.
For you will feel me, right up to the hilt.

THE FULL EXTENT

What is it about you, darling?
What is it about you that drives me so crazy?
Is it your name? The glorious handful of letters
that were put together for me
to repeat over and over like an incantation?
Is it your eyes?
The rich hues of which
have reflected the light and wonder of my own.
Is it your lips? The full and perfect pair
that whisper requests to me in my very dreams;
leaving even my subconscious
with a desire to ravage you.
I don't know what it is, darling.
I can't quite put my finger on it,
without wanting to slip that same finger inside.
Wishing to warm that one place
that hardens men like steel,
and makes gods out of mortals.
It isn't fair
knowing that you get to
walk around and draw breath,
as you ache for me in secret.
While I sit here with the rising proof of my cravings,
waiting for you to relieve me of such a state.
You will pay for these transgressions, my love.
Your penance shall be deeply paid,
when your legs adorn my shoulders,
and it feels like there are more
than butterflies in your stomach.
You will know then,
the full extent of my love for you.
And in turn, you will be free to come undone,
as we both are purified in the flames
we have done our best to tame.
Never has failure felt better...
Wouldn't you agree?

CLYDE HURLSTON

OVERDUE REUNION

It remains lodged inside the stone,
as the legends once foretold.
Waiting impatiently for your divine hand
to arrive and take a hold.
For only you could ensure its release,
and wield its unbridled power.
And use it slay our collective demons,
during each transcendent hour.
Of course this is just a dream,
since chaos conspires to fill your days.
Still, i long for our overdue reunion;
so i can hear as this hardened blade,
takes your breath away.

GODDESS WORSHIP

Friend, I often go to church,
but it's when my doors are closed.
For my place in Heaven is truly found,
when she removes her robes.
Her every curve is a Revelation,
that's sure to make me praise.
She smiles as she sees the monolith,
that desire helped me raise.
And it only grows in size,
the closer that she gets.
I'll say au revoir to sorrows now,
and adios to my regrets.
For safety often comes to me,
in a form both humble and divine.
And I feel redeemed by the truth,
since I can call her mine.
But now she straddles me,
and all my thoughts are lost.
Then we share the deepest kiss,
and I feel my restraint exhaust.
As I feel my fire rise,
the demons start to dance.
Knowing that angels often blush,
when near such a carnal circumstance.
Now she's slowly sliding down,
to be impaled upon my love.
Now transcendence can begin,
I thank my stars above.
Her moans become a symphony,
played to an audience of one.
Her demands must be met,
until this ritual is done.
Now her hands are in my hair,

CLYDE HURLSTON

as mine roughly squeezed her ass.
It feels like destruction and rebirth,
as these sacred minutes pass.
But then I can take no more,
and I fill her form of paradise.
With liquid proof of all my love,
her legs enclose me like a vise.
Then she collapses into my arms,
where she is safe and sound
And we'll both sleep until we feel,
it's time to go another round.

BLOOM

Darling, I often imagine how you'll sound,
the moment I first enter your garden.
Will you welcome me with whispers?
Or will your moans echo like thunder?
For with each subsequent thrust,
I feel the clouds swell as they gather rain.
Still, I take comfort knowing
my storms will not pour,
until you have had
more than one chance to bloom.

CLYDE HURLSTON

STORM THE CASTLE

An impressive sword unsheathed
Takes but seconds to disappear.
And the delightful sounds you make
Are received like music by my ears.
For the blade buried in your garden
Will cause it to do everything but wilt
Oh, I love to see your expressions
As you take it right up to the hilt.
Darling, when all is said and done,
I will be the one to blame.
And when I ask who it belongs to,
I expect to hear my name.
Because I aim to give you pleasure
And maybe just a little pain.
So you can crown me as your King,
As I storm your castle,
For as long as I can reign.

THE COLLECTIVE FATE OF STARS

Darling, I am often left speechless
when I reminisce over our time together.
Though it was brief,
the power we unleashed
in those moments of passion,
helped me to understand
the process in which stars collapse.
I would wager that even the gods
loved to watch all we did
to one another on those nights.
For you were the spark
that woke the eternal flame within, my love.
It was your kiss that would resurrect my spirit.
It was your touch that effortlessly raised
the monument I kept for you.
And once you removed your clothes,
it was then that all bets were off.
From the moment you first let me inside,
we both knew that going supernova
was in our collective destiny.
Yet, as I sift through these memories,
I'm still left to wonder
exactly where the old me would go.
Because with you, I became someone else.
All of the doubt and insecurity was gone.
There was only the desire to please you,
intertwined with a once dormant hunger
and a lustful rage.
Though I always understood,
I truthfully resented the amount of time
you'd make me wait to see you.
And so, I wasn't satisfied
until you felt every place that I'd been

CLYDE HURLSTON

for days after we had parted.
With each thrust you endured,
the demons grew more and more silent;
allowing me to focus on doing
whatever was necessary
for us to explode together.

ON A CLOUD

You would always tell me
that I worried too much.
And I guess it was because
putting pressure on myself
was what I did best
besides loving you, darling.
I just always felt like my best
wasn't quite good enough.
I was an imperfect man seeking perfection.
An artist who was barely a novice,
seeking to create a masterpiece.
In my eyes, you deserved no less.
Attempting to reach the unattainable
was the least I could do,
after you had given yourself to me.
For how can you repay someone
for a gift that cannot be bought?
How can that without a price
ever truly be quantified?
And so, I felt my best effort
was all I had to give you.
Where other men wanted
to leave you with a smile,
I always sought to leave you on a cloud.
So I would place this humble tongue
within your garden,
and speak the language of the gods
until you barely remembered your own name.
I would fight with everything I had,
so that this monument you raised
would not rival Pompeii with its explosions,
until I had thoroughly explored every corner
of your temple from the inside.

CLYDE HURLSTON

I wanted my name to decorate
the breaths between your moans,
as I thrusted with purpose
and made myself at home.
And for the rest of my days,
I will pray that when you close your eyes
in the still of the night,
you can still feel the places I've been
and know I was the reason
the moon would come with tides.

EXAMINE THE STARS

At night, I venture into dreams,
to escape the loneliness of life.
Though I don't always recall them when I wake,
the thought of you still lingers, darling.
And I'm lost in a haze of expectation,
as I imagine what it will be like
to kiss you for the very first time.
The anticipation of our lips colliding,
for what shall be
a moment of transcendence,
leaves me cursing the hands of time;
and their cruelest of decisions
to make us wait.
For it is through your passion,
that I long to rediscover
my fondness for weightlessness.
I know your love will take me out of this world,
and oh baby, I am ready to go.
My things are all but packed;
but I swear I won't carry any baggage
with me into your arms.
I will be yours, and yours alone,
if you'll have me.
I pray you'll grant me the permission
to make my home inside of you.
I will search until I find
the deepest places I will fit,
all in the effort of
reminding you who your were;
before your feet first touched the ground.
Give yourself to me, baby,
and we will examine the stars;
after I finally discover how sweet you taste.

CLYDE HURLSTON

HOLDING ON TO LET GO

Lay down your armor, darling.
I assure you, weapons are not needed
inside these castle walls.
Believe me, I know how dangerous
the outside world can be.
But deep down,
you know you have nothing to fear from me.
If I did not want you here,
you would have never made it past the door.
And if you did not want me,
surely your clothing
would not be lying upon the floor.
We both know exactly why
you are here, my love.
I am the place you come
to when you need to cum.
I am that which you hold on to,
when you are dying
to let go of everything else.
After you have been forced
to throw down the gauntlet
just to get your goals accomplished,
it is my honor to lie down beneath you
and throw you down upon my hardened love.
When your only desire
is to finally let your hair down,
I feel it is my duty
to take it in my hand and pull,
as I ravage you from behind.
And when you have tired
of carrying this world upon your shoulders,
I will lay you down,
so that I may put your legs upon mine.

THE SACRED GIFT OF FIRE

Oh, darling, you are mine until I am done.
Only after you have been made to surrender,
will you be set free.
Only after you exhale your concerns
and sweat out your sorrows,
will you be allowed to leave.
I say this knowing my bed
will never be your cage:
but when I am in this state,
I must proudly be your mage.
Ensuring that your cares will swiftly disappear,
one hard thrust at a time.

CLYDE HURLSTON

EFFECTS OF THE MOON

When I think about it now,
I'm sure you knew exactly
what you were doing, darling.
You stepped off that plane,
with every intention
of waking the beast within me.
It had been years since a woman
had me counting the minutes until I saw her.
And with each passing second,
I grew more impatient;
ever the more selfish.
You were going to pay the cost
for all of the time I spent waiting for you.
And from the first second I was inside you,
the sounds you made
proved the full moon wasn't the only thing
that could bring about the change in a man.
I watched the soft flesh on your hips redden,
as my hands grabbed them
to hold you exactly where I fucking wanted you.
And from the first thrust,
the walls within you proved no match for my love.
I imagined you began
to sympathize with the lost city of Jericho,
as I began to explore other angles of entry.
As your legs began to shake,
I was certain that you enjoyed being at my mercy.
You always found power in surrendering to me.
And that night, I rediscovered my own
by impaling you with every inch of my love,
until you said my name with religious reverence.

MY INTENSE EFFORTS

If I got to fuck her
as often as I have
written about her,
I could have changed
the way she walked.
And come to think of it,
if that was the case,
these pages wouldn't be
the only things
that were left wet
from my intense efforts.

CLYDE HURLSTON

SOUTHERN GIRL

"There's nothing like a southern girl,"
I once told my friend with pride.
"She can take any man to Heaven's gate,
If she let you deep inside.
But not every man will get a pass,
Unless they prove they're up to snuff.
And if she sees they're well-equipped,
She may demand you give it rough.
And you'll know she's a southern girl,
If you're beneath her as she rides.
Up and down with grace and ease,
Hell, she's the envy of the tides.
And then you'd feel that southern girl,
As she increased her speed.
As if to show she'd lost control,
Once you hit the spot she needs.
And if you struggle to hold on,
You can grab her southern curves.
Just have your actions match your word,
And be the man that she deserves.
You'll thank God she's a southern girl,
When her mouth does more than pray.
She's got the skills to take your soul,
But she'll only take your cares away.
Yeah there's not much that she won't do,
If you prove to be a man that she can trust.
Believe me, friend, it's the southern girls
That helped to make a man of us."

EXPLORE:HER

In the recent years,
I have developed
a voracious appetite for discovery.
Though I am reticent to admit,
I am so rarely given the chance
to explore that which matters most: her.
While it is true, I have inscribed my name
into a few holy places in my time;
I always imagined venturing into her garden
when I thought of home.
For I knew the waters there
would turn a molehill into a mountain;
with the irony being
that every time she reached the summit,
would be seconds after
she took my love to the base.
Because it has been far too long
since her gates were held open
and even bent back,
until she could feel my return
in the depths of her very soul.
And judging by the look
that usually adorned her face,
the only thing better than her wetness
causing me to fall out of Grace,
was the shared ecstasy
of my re-entry into Eden.
Over and over again.

CLYDE HURLSTON

ON SUNDAY MORNING

It had felt like forever since I was with a woman.
And this time I was reunited with
one of the few who knew me best.
She would say that she has never been
a practitioner of magic;
although she recalled each of the rituals
that woke the selfish beast in me.
And she performed each of them with an eagerness,
I had not seen in years.
For it was with her soft hands and skilled mouth
that she proved time had not dulled her memory;
rather it only increased her appetite for pleasing me.
And when the time arrived for her to welcome home
the monument she raised, she would spare no second
nor would she leave any inch to the elements.
She somehow took it all.
And as she repeatedly called out my name,
as if it were her favorite incantation,
I began to wonder to myself:
"Is this what God feels like on Sunday morning?"

QUAND IL ENTRA AU PARADIS

Tell me, darling...
could you see the stars
when your eyes rolled back into your head?
Does it surprise you to know
that I can remember every sound you made,
when I first entered your temple?
Inch by inch, you welcomed me;
all the way down to the base,
joining us at the soul.
You belonged to me from that moment forth;
I was too deep for you to say otherwise.
And with your legs upon my shoulders,
being bent back towards you,
you weren't in a position
to do anything but come undone.
I watched you grasp for the sheets
as if they were a last lifeline,
as I unleashed the beast that you made me.
You were so wet that I slipped out,
leaving your eyes fighting tears
as if I had fallen from grace.
But your despair was all for naught,
as I entered you again;
proving that the only thing better
than my time inside, was each re-entry.

CLYDE HURLSTON

STOP AND SMELL THE ROSES

My mind keeps demanding that I stop,
As if there were roses here to smell.
And not a subtle kind of precipice,
Into which I had already fell.
And since there's no reason good enough,
I'll resume my chosen path to tread.
Yet since I have never found my way to another's heart,
This uncertainty is breeding dread.
So tell me if I am wrong to doubt,
Or even question if you're true?
Or should I focus on the laundry list of things,
that I wish you'd let me do to you?
For I've ravaged you a thousand times,
Behind these windows to my soul.
And to make that dream a reality,
Is my only honest goal.
I need to worship at the temple,
You have hidden well beneath your clothes.
Won't you let my hands caress your petals,
Until it was a part of me that rose?
Because if you would let me, darling,
Oh, I would fill you completely.

BETWEEN THE LINES

Here my lonely fingers go,
Caressing this page again.
Having been denied the luxury,
Of exploring the glory of your skin.
Still, they fit so much between the lines
You'd think they'd run out of space.
But it's amazing how certain things can grow,
By just imagining your face.
And my mind seems so eager to recall
All the things we used to do.
Like the way your body used to shake
When my quill reached deep inside of you
I reveled in the way you'd take it all
As you begged this writer not to stop
For you loved the debt I paid with ink
And you longed to feel my every drop.

CLYDE HURLSTON

THE DEPTHS LOVE COULD REACH

Your warm embrace
was all that was expected, darling.
A simple hug to say goodbye
after a wonderful evening.
But that's not all that happened, was it, baby?
No, I still remember what happened next
as if it were yesterday.
I can still feel your soft hands
grabbing my large face as you began to kiss me.
As if you were demanding me to stay
without saying a single word.
And it was a kiss that haunts me to this very day.
Because I can see now, looking back,
how much courage it took for you to do that.
And you'll never know how many nights
I wished I never had to leave afterwards.
You'll never know how many times I couldn't sleep,
because I was imagining all of the things
I wish I would have done to you that night.
I wanted to leave you sore
in places your hands couldn't reach.
I wanted to fill you with the kind of passion
you had only read about, but never felt for yourself.
Darling, I wanted to fuck you so well,
you'd have no choice but to love me.
But things didn't work out that way;
for a myriad of reasons.
Still, I can't help but wonder at times,
how these words would feel to you,
if only you had first felt
the depths my love could reach.

A CASTLE STORMED

She had spent so many
sleepless nights building walls,
that she began to feel like a prisoner
in a castle of her own making.
The moats that swelled at the bottoms of her eyes
served as warnings to potential intruders;
implying that she would drown them all,
should they misstep.
Choosing to spend her days in isolation,
this reluctant queen forsook the fairy tales;
having labeled them as merely the products
of a child's imagination.
But on this night, her Knight was found.
And in turn, she became the castle
that was stormed and plundered.
His love for her having been
demonstrated by his siege,
he overwhelmed her with a passion
birthed from an intensity that felt like war.
She was powerless to stop herself.
As inhibitions and regrets fell from her mind
like the stones of crumbling walls,
all she could do now
was surrender to the feeling.
And as his love penetrated
even her deepest corners,
she knew that not only
had her reign just begun...
she had found the one
that would rule beside her; and inside her.
For all her days to come.

CLYDE HURLSTON

FORCE OF NATURE

Like a force of nature she came,
into a world that I left unprepared.
She was said to leave wreckage in her wake,
but I was so lonely I rarely ever cared.
Yet she had a way of soothing,
all these thoughts inside my head.
And there were things that she could do,
that left my inner beast quite content and fed.
Yet heavy winds and rain tore red flags off the mast,
before they could ever reach my eyes.
Still, her legs often found my shoulders,
when they weren't spread into the skies.
So my friend, I cannot pretend that I did not enjoy,
these things we did of our own accord.
But at night, I often wonder why,
she was the very first storm that I ever swam toward.

WHEN CAN WE START?

On nights like this,
I can't help but think of you.
I know I'm not supposed to
steer my mind in your direction;
but to hell with all these rules.
Tonight, you'll be mine.
I'll have you behind my eyes,
even if that's the only place we will ever meet.
It takes very little to get me started.
I close my eyes for a second,
and already I'm drunk off of your perfume.
I didn't think it was possible
for me to want you anymore than I do;
but here I am, far past the point of no return.
Now I need to know if you taste better than you look.
And after I've had my fill,
I have every intention of filling you.
For I need to know how you can take me,
once you've seen how hard you make me.
Darling, what does it do to you to know this?
To know you put the motion in my hand;
and not only when I'm writing.
Do you imagine my large hand around your throat,
holding you in place?
As you feel this part of me reach places
your last lover couldn't find, even if he had a map?
It pains me to know what you settled for...
Just as it now pains you to know,
how my form of worship can leave you sore.
I need you to feel where I've been,
days after I am gone.
So that you know
I've been telling the truth all along.

CLYDE HURLSTON

The only thing I'll be better at than writing
is fucking you properly.
Practice makes perfect, baby.
And after I'm finished making a mess tonight,
all I'll need to know from you is:
When can we start?

SANCTUARIES

With cathedrals crushed beneath
The weight of false pretense
I find the actions of a few
Lacking adequate defense
For each truth I held as prayer
Has now been proven false
Still, my sinful sanctuary
Possesses breath and pulse
So I must venture to the East
Letting each solstice point the way
For our alignments are too rare
Since she chooses not to stay
And here I have unearthed
Desires I once thought were dead
That mirror all the ungodly things
I have often wrote or said
Yet perfection is unattainable
When the vessel is shaped like mine
But I find efforts bathed in sweat
Are themselves worthy of a rhyme.

LOSE CONTROL

Can I paint a pretty picture
And let the colors coalesce?
As I imagine beads of sweat
Raining off your perfect breasts
I watch you rise and fall
As if you were the sea
Each time you wear surprise
As if you can't believe
Just how deep inside
This hardened love can reach
Invading castles made of sand
Upon your internal beach
Now my hands will take your hips
And they will hold them still
For there are inhibitions left in you
I won't stop until I kill
And with each forceful thrust
I feel you come undone
That's it, now take it all
Oh my darling, don't you run
Because you know there is no need
For you to wipe your eyes
You know you're always safe with me
So it is okay to cry
If you have never felt this good
In what has felt like years
As long as you don't succumb
To all your doubts and fears
Here my only aim, my love
Is to reach your soul
So you can't start taking charge
Until I've first made you lose control.

WITH UNSEEN HUES

Today, the memories came flooding back,
and I remembered my short time as an artist.
I was surely an awkward, humble man; but
I was on my way to becoming a master.
A budding Rembrandt, that was commissioned
to work exclusively for one.
And that one was her: my Queen;
my living work of art.
For me, our time together
was the envy of the Renaissance.
I recalled with pride as her legs
adorned my shoulders like armor;
and with each brushstroke of this tongue,
I painted masterpieces in her garden.
Oh, how her exquisite canvas
would rise and fall like the tides,
absorbing all I had to give.
Her hands would dance within my hair,
all the while pulling my face deeper into her color.
Ensuring that I continued painting
with unseen hues of love;
proving that her starving artist was truly Famished.
Her approval of my work, expressed in breaths
that sounded like Symphonies;
for a time I loved in the fashion of the gods.
But such a thing was not meant to last forever;
rather it was made to be displayed
in the gallery of my mind, until my final breath.

CLYDE HURLSTON

SMOKE AFTER READING

Every time I sit down to write,
Before I even pick up my pen,
I first imagine your response.
I picture you there
Biting your perfect lips
And waiting with bated breath.
Eager to see,
If you can find yourself between these lines.
And as your eyes pour over that first line,
It's like those first few moments of penetration.
You can't help but let out a gasp,
As you take all that I have to offer.
All the way to the base.
Each sentence becoming another thrust.
I'm getting deep now, baby.
Have I reached your soul?
Oh, that's right…
You don't remember how to speak.
All you can do is read.
Pretending each phrase I turn,
Is just another position I've put you in.
You close your eyes
As the sounds of our flesh colliding
Echoes in your mind.
You're getting closer now.
So you open your eyes to re-read each line;
Over and over again.
You never do want me to stop,
Do you, darling?
Not once I really get going.
But I must admit
It's getting harder to hold it in, babe.
I need you to finish before I do.

THE SACRED GIFT OF FIRE

Yeah, that's it.
That's my good girl.
Show me you can take it all.
And that's when you reach
The bottom of the page
And realize that I'm not there with you.
Yet, you smile for me.
Knowing that even though
We've yet to actually touch,
I've been inside of you all along.

CLYDE HURLSTON

THE OCEAN

Darling,
what is it about the ocean,
that brings our love to mind?
Is it because we're a force of nature,
whenever we're entwined?
Or is it the way the tide pounds the shore,
and leaves it wanting more?
The same way I do for you,
until you're satisfied and sore.

TRAJECTORY

She once told me
that seeing my name
flash across her phone,
could change the trajectory of her day.
Now I can't help but imagine
how good she will feel.
with her legs on my shoulders,
as I'm pounding all of her stress away.

OTHERWORLDLY

She had absolutely no idea
how fucking good it feels to be inside of her.
I could scream the words from mountaintops,
and the echoes might as well be whispers.
For part of me grows with the mere thought of her.
So how on Earth do you describe
something this transcendent and do it justice?
It's impossible to do.
And despite having a way with words,
I am often left speechless
when I think about having my way with her.
Yet in the moment,
the only thing that escapes my lips are commands.
I am primal when it comes to pleasing her.
Timid men have no business between her legs.
So that is why I demand
that she taste herself upon my love.
Maybe then she will learn what it's like,
having something otherworldly upon her tongue.

SYLLABLES & STANZAS

With the blatant movements of my hand,
The words seemed to come alive.
I imagined my every line became a thrust,
Until I left her with stanzas in her eyes.
And as each couplet was bathed in tears,
She seemed to be overwhelmed at times.
Drifting beyond pure joy into ecstasy
Her body began to shake,
And leave her juices on my rhymes.
So I continued with my writing still
My hand now increasing with its speed
While hoping that the depth inside each syllable
Would help me give her every single thing she'd need
And as she asked for proof she was the muse
I felt my explosion was getting close
For dancing in my mind were the images
Of her, the woman that I have wanted most.

CLYDE HURLSTON

HEAVEN & EARTH

It's that time again, my love.
Time for us to be but proof
for the Principles that we adore.
I have been without you for too long, now.
So only our most sacred union will do.
I fear I am much too worked up for you,
so we will have to engage in this hieros gamos
without the pomp or ceremony.
Still, as we come together,
Heaven & Earth doth smile upon us.
For as it is above,
so mote there be below.
And as the impressive root of my love
enters your reflection of Eden,
is there any surprise that waters flow for me?
Yes, that is what I need, darling.
Baptize my love here and now,
and by the gods, I will rain for you.

READ & WONDER

Darling, I have left you
ample space between these lines.
The doors to the reservoir have long been open.
The last entrant wasn't brave enough to stay.
And she never closed the door behind her.
So it is now open to you.
But I can sense the uneasiness in you.
Still worried about what the others will say.
Fearing I am not what is expected for you to love.
So you hide this effect I have on you.
All the while, you read these words
while biting your lip.
Knowing damn well,
these lines do more than get you wet;
they make you curse the dry land.
For it is within this world I've woven,
that you wish to bathe.
It is within the depths of my growing lust,
that you wish to drown.
But still, you won't give yourself to me.
You're content to simply read and wonder;
forgetting there will be a brave soul,
who lets me take her under.

CLYDE HURLSTON

THE SOUND OF GRATITUDE

It had been too damn long
since I had seen her last;
And needless to say,
I was past impatient at this point.
My excitement was clearly visible;
and I don't even mean upon my face.
She does this to me, every single time.
She goes to say something,
but the time for talking is done now.
With my large hand on each side of her face,
I kiss her so hard,
I drink the words that
she was attempting to speak.
She looks up at me;
content and breathless.
Then I simply point to the bed.
By now she knows exactly what I want.
She bends over the bed and reaches under
to take me into her temple.
With every single thrust,
she pays the primal cost of my waiting.
She has no choice
but to take what I have for her.
In between her bites of the bedsheets,
I thought I heard her praying.
But what she was actually doing
was whispering to me over and over:
"Thank you. Thank you."
And I smiled.
For I've always loved the sound
of gratitude in a woman.
Especially one
that isn't afraid to belong to me.

WE MADE MUSIC

To me, her every moan was a gift.
A present earned and unwrapped
with each subsequent thrust.
My God, she was so alive in these moments.
The look in her eyes? Electric.
And as our passions increased,
things began to intensify.
That's when she began to change.
All of this time, she had been holding on...
To the bedsheets, to me,
to anything she could reach.
But now, she was letting go.
I watched her unleash
all that she had been hiding within.
And her moans began to sound like notes
in a song that she sang just for me.
As if by going as deeply as I did,
I had earned myself a symphony.
The sounds of our flesh colliding
began performing duets with a soundtrack
of much-deserved spanks
and sternly given commands.
She simply couldn't get enough.
For every time she trembled,
I stood more firmly inside of her.
Proving that on some nights we fucked.
On others, we made love.
But tonight?
Tonight was the night that we made music.

CLYDE HURLSTON

WELCOME HOME

I only had to look into your eyes
to know you were ready.
I could tell from your silence,
from your impatient breathing,
that you've been waiting as long as I have.
The only difference being
you've been waiting for your chance to escape;
and I've been waiting for you
to remember exactly where you belong.
And tonight, that will be any place I put you.
I'm so starved for you,
I almost don't know where to begin.
Almost.
There is only thing a man can do
when he is Famished, and that is to eat.
So I bend you over
and begin tasting you from behind.
Using the grace in my tongue,
to prepare your temple for my offering.
And when I can wait no longer,
I stand and enter you as slowly as possible.
All the way to the base.
Ah, you remember don't you, my love?
The first stroke was short,
since I knew you'd want them long.
By the second stroke,
your legs were not as strong.
By the third stroke,
I made you regret the time that you were gone.
And by the fourth stroke you called me god,
and simply whispered: "Welcome Home."

A CAVEMAN'S KIND OF LOVE

Does the thought of my hand around your throat,
put the motion in your own?
Have you ever imagined finding your release,
while hearing my voice upon the phone?
Do you send yourself to sleep,
hoping to be taken in a dream?
Have you buried your face inside the bed,
so others wouldn't hear you as you scream?
Have you chosen to misbehave,
just to receive the consequence?
Are you willing to then receive,
or do you resist with false pretense?
Darling, when it comes to love,
can I thrust my way to trust?
Shall I bury it inside,
and watch you struggle to adjust?
Will these handfuls of your hair,
help you forget your every care?
Should I tie you to the bed,
so you don't have to wonder what to wear?
Should I cover up your pretty eyes,
so you're blind to all my plans?
Or should I place you on your knees,
and let you beg to service my demands?
Maybe I've treated you far too kind,
And made you a goddess in my mind.
When I should've given you a caveman's kind of love,
and only destroyed you from behind.
Now you'll shut up and take what I have to give.

CLYDE HURLSTON

WHAT YOU'VE BEEN MISSING

My memories are running on fumes.
It seems that I've gotten high
off of them for so long,
only the vapors remain.
But since we have started talking again,
I find the daydreams arrive more frequently.
Visions of our long, overdue reunion.
Oh, darling, my desire for you
Is pouring through my thoughts like gasoline.
And at this point,
just the word hello from you could ignite me.
Hell, I still have yet to hear your voice again.
God only knows, what I'm going to do
when I hear my name
decorate the space between your moans.
As I raise and lower your perfect frame,
down upon my love.
Each time, filling you up
and allowing you to feel me
all the way to the base.
You haven't hurt this good
in a long time, have you, baby?
I know. It's okay.
We have the rest of our days
for you to receive
exactly what you have been missing.
As deep and as often as you can take it.

UNFORGETTABLE PENMANSHIP

From the beginning,
my pen had piqued your curiosity.
Then with each subsequent piece,
you stopped being able to help yourself.
And that is when your attention
began to belong to me.
Just as you eventually would;
despite what you may have once planned.
And now that lay you spread out before me,
with your impatience decorating the air between us.
You're dying to know if my pen writes reality,
aren't you, darling?
Well after just the tip of this pen
had made its way inside,
you had to wonder no more.
You knew I wrote only truth.
For I would now do to you,
what I had done to so many a page:
I would have my way with you.
Until only a beautiful mess was left behind.
You worried if your margins
could contain all I had to offer;
but I was so deep at this point, you didn't care.
You just didn't want me to stop.
Not until you had reached the summit.
And not until I was finished writing
my masterpiece within you.
It's a shame I didn't believe in myself sooner.
I could have been doing this from the very start.
Who knew that all this time
I was capable of such unforgettable penmanship?
Oh, that's right... you did.

TWO CARELESS SHIPS (PART 1 OF 2)

On an altar made of satin,
I aimed to sacrifice her fears.
Inhibitions were never welcome,
through seconds that felt like years.
Without clothes she laid before me,
in a glory seldom ever seen.
She bid me to come toward her,
so I knew this had to be a dream.
But I walked forward all the same,
she smiled, knowing that I would.
I placed her legs upon my shoulders,
and entered her temple as deeply as I could.
I heard a gasp escape her lips,
a breathless request followed soon.
She softly begged me not to stop,
and I become her beast beneath the moon.
In a rush, I'd lift her off the altar,
and pressed her against the wall.
My hands held her ass so tightly,
her heart was the only thing to fall.
I threw her down upon my love,
as her nails made homes inside my neck.
We were lost in our desires,
so two careless ships were bound to wreck.
Our collision produced explosions,
that were the envy of the stars.
For even supernovas had to bow,
when they witnessed a passion displayed like ours.
And she kissed my lips so deeply,
I tasted prayers she never said.
As "How long before we can go again?"
was ringing loudly in my head.

MIRROR THE SEA (PART 2 OF 2)

Through the black silk of her robe,
there are hints as to what she has in store for me.
With the pull of a string, I am blessed to see
her temple in all of its glory.
Such a thing makes a man
feel lucky to be alive.
As she moves toward me,
I realize that I am now bare before her.
With every inch she advances,
my love proudly grows to greet her.
She slowly sits on top of me,
with the grace of queen taking her throne.
As she kisses me,
deep enough to exchange our greetings unspoken;
I exhale my inhibitions like smoke.
Through that haze she reaches down,
and places me inside of her.
I'm so deep that I prepare myself to drown,
as she begins to mirror the sea.
Rising up and crashing down upon my love like waves,
I swear I can begin to feel her soul.
The magical sounds she makes
leave me drunk in disbelief.
I marvel at her work,
as she ravages the obelisk upon my shore.
Grabbing her hips, I thrust upward,
hoping to catch her.
And as her body begins to shake,
I watch as she screams without breath,
and she falls without fear.
Safely into my arms.

FARAWAY EYES

With each grain that falls,
a man grows impatient.
Failing to learn the lessons of the masters,
he finds himself
stumbling drunk on memories.
Only this time,
it is not the distant past that haunts him;
but rather, experiences
fresh enough to taste.
The cinnamon still ripe upon her lips,
the hunger pouring out of her eyes...
He doesn't have to imagine
being desired anymore.
She has not only made it known,
she has put words to action.
And as her body
welcomed him into her grace,
they began to write their tales anew.
As she climbed on top of him,
his quill reached deep
into her reservoir of emotions;
scraping at the edges of her soul.
His large, right hand
wrapped around her throat,
his left hand guiding her hips;
he thrusted upward
and wrote her into ecstasy.
Each time she flashed her faraway eyes,
their bodies struck each other
like the lashes of a whip.
More was not enough.
And now time spent apart is agony;
until they meet again.

SORCERESS

It was clear from the look in her eyes,
That this would be no ordinary night.
But I wasn't in a mindspace
That would allow me to get excited over anything.
Still, I knew she was up to something.
Because every single thing she said,
Could easily be taken another way.
And every time she touched me,
Her hands lingered just a little too long.
That's when she leaned in
And began to undo my belt:
I knew I was in trouble then.
And I'd been alone so long,
I forgot what a sorceress she could be.
How else could you explain
Her being able to entice a man with no hope,
And easily raising his monument with no rope?
She was far too skilled for this to be chance.
And so I simply held her hair,
And watched her begin this seance upon my love.
Who knew that once the moon was full,
It would be me that she drained?

CLYDE HURLSTON

MADE TO HOWL

From the look in her eyes,
I knew it was on.
She didn't have to say a word.
With the intensity of that first kiss,
it was clear she didn't plan
on being a lady tonight.
She was a love-starved wolf
That would be made to fucking howl.....
Or else.
And it seems that neither of us
could get undressed fast enough.
Still, we stood in our natural state
around the same time.
Before I could even sit on the edge of the bed,
she sharply inhaled and took me in her mouth.
I kept thinking that she had to be a witch,
how else could she make
the whole thing disappear like that?
And it wasn't long before her impatience grew
larger than she made my love.
That's when I laid back and watched her
impale herself upon the sword once held in stone.
Each time, she would throw herself down harder
and the louder she would moan.
I was afraid she was going to hurt herself
since I was deep enough to kill her demons.
But it was clear that was her goal.
I was just honored to be the man she chose,
once she was ready to finally lose control.
Because she knew how much I loved her.

WHEN THE DEVIL INSPIRES PRAYER

Darling,
The only thing I miss more than loving you,
Is being able to please you.
Because, for me,
The only place that felt better
Than sleeping beside you
Was being inside you.
My God, this pen cannot convey
The way it felt every single time
You allowed me to enter Eden.
There are never enough lines
To express the way
Your moans became incantations,
And summoned the Famished beast I became.
And each time my love reached its base,
I could hear you getting closer to the summit.
Oh baby, I wanted you to reach up
And pull down the goddamn stars.
Maybe then you would understand
The heat I withstood
As I reached new depths within you;
And forced myself
To hold on just a little longer.
Because I couldn't allow myself
To explode until you had gone
Supernova more than once.
Whilst praising the human devil,
That makes you call out for God.

CLYDE HURLSTON

FROM SYMPHONIES TO SILENCE

The silence has echoed
For far too long now!
It has been years
Since I heard my favorite song:
The unmistakable sounds
Of your rapturous moans
As they were accompanied
by our flesh colliding.
As the force of each thrust
Sent ripples across your perfect skin,
I tried to reach further into you
So that our symphony might continue
Just a little bit longer.
Do you have any idea what it's like
Trying to ensure that the crescendo isn't reached
During the overture, darling?
Have you any idea the strength it takes
To endure your movements
And not lose myself within the first sonata?
I must be a disciplined conductor, my love.
How else could I maintain
The rhythm that you need
To reach your personal summit?
Anything less would be unacceptable to me.
To not reach our denouement together,
Would be nothing less than heresy.
Still, all I have left of you now are memories.
I pray to the gods,
You will return one day.
Bringing the music back
To a life that has fallen
Painfully silent without you.

THE FOUR ELEMENTS

I'm sure as they have chosen
to read these words I've left behind,
some will come to wonder
why I was so in love with you.
And it's quite simple, darling:
in those times we were together,
we were able to discover the four elements.
Despite what your silence says now,
during those times we were clandestine
and hid from the world,
we were the envy of the alchemists.
For just one look
deep into each other's eyes produced the Fire.
After any time apart,
that first kiss upon reunion,
stole the Air from each other's lungs.
And let us not forget
that every time you allowed me inside of you,
the Earth moved with each subsequent thrust.
Which allowed your garden
to then produce its holy Water,
to ensure you could take all of my offering.
And after each time I slipped out,
I wonder if the gods delighted in seeing
just how ravenous you were
for my re-entry into Eden.
For they surely knew
my aim was to reach the forge in your very soul.
So that I could explode within it
and transmute all that we shared into gold.
But such a thing is better left
between these lines now, my love.
For you have moved on as you always have.

CLYDE HURLSTON

Always settling for what is next,
rather than what is right.
And make no mistake, such is your choice.
But just know, there will come a time
when another takes your place within my heart.
And after she has taken
my firmest element to its base,
we will both reach new heights of ecstasy.
And the air up there
will not smell of regret, but of love.
And with that view amongst the clouds,
it will be hard to see that you ever existed at all.

THE SPECTER OF OPPORTUNITY

In my dreams, the planets converged
when our bodies would merge, darling.
There behind my eyes,
there were no doubts.
No insecurities. No signals to be misinterpreted.
And certainly, no performance anxieties.
There, in that timeless dimension of thought,
there was only us.
There, we had no place else to be.
No phone calls to be answered.
No last-minute errands to be run.
All that mattered then was pleasure.
And raising it to the level of ecstasy.
Because unlike most souls,
I never took this act for granted.
I always believed it to be a privilege.
And I suspect that is why
the specter of missed opportunities
always loomed so large in my imagination.
For I knew, deep down in my soul,
there were new discoveries to be made.
I hadn't yet even scratched the surface
of what I was capable of giving to another soul.
I knew that beneath my own uncertainty and timidity,
something greater was waiting to emerge.
And I wanted that actualized version
of whatever I was to become,
to perfect all the ways
that I could make you cum, my love.
For I would not be satisfied
until I brought you back to life
better than you were, before your every little death.

CLYDE HURLSTON

IN SERVICE OF THE KING

She said she wanted to be the one
that put the motion in my wrist;
yet she didn't mean to write.
Rather she was referring to when I was alone,
inside my humble bed at night.
She wished to bestow unto me an urge,
that I was unable to control.
The kind where an epic mess upon release,
is the result of this myopic goal.
So she sought to become a fabled muse,
and earn her place between my lines.
Claiming that she would not be just another rose,
that chose to overlook the vines.
That she is when she often called my name,
and let it dance upon her breath.
With intentions of introducing loneliness,
to its god-forsaken death.
And that is when she took some photographs,
with clever placement of the lens.
Seeking to entice and still maintain,
our status as "only friends."
Still, she sought to raise the monument,
that only a few lucky souls had seen.
Because she wished to become the centerpiece,
of my most lustful, vivid dreams.
But what this goddess failed to realize,
is that I'm no longer sated by a tease.
For on this path to sovereignty,
I will only make an effort to be pleased.
And if hands and lips are not offered up,
in service to this would-be king.
Then my lines must be held in reserve for the queen,
who will become my everything.

THE SACRED GIFT OF FIRE

And not someone who only speaks,
when it's attention that she craves.
I prefer a woman who invokes a passion that,
will make us both its slaves.
But such a soul is rare indeed,
and so for her sake I must withhold.
For my ink is gold I will not waste,
on a woman who will not help me to explode.

CLYDE HURLSTON

FILLED WITH GRATITUDE

Her encouragement of me
always went a long way.
But recently, her temptation
allowed me to go a little farther.
For we had spoken of history,
and also discussed the present tense.
But for what she showed me next,
I had prepared little to no defense.
So there was no way to resist,
and the difficulty could be seen.
And I would rival Pompeii on this day,
by re-enacting its most famous scene.
And she discovered one of many ways,
I could possibly be inspired.
And as she went about her day,
I only hope she felt desired.
For her support has meant the world,
and this gift meant even more.
Now I'm left anticipating those,
other revelations she has in store.
And someday we will be face to face,
then I'll be able to thank her properly.
By filling her dripping depths with gratitude,
whether she's folded up beneath
or placed on top of me.

UNDER THE RIGHT CONDITIONS

While standing at the kitchen counter,
my lover said: "you'll have to forgive me, babe.
I'm moving slower than usual today."
"Even if the movement is slow,
under the right conditions,
friction can cause fires all the same, darling."
I replied, as I began pressing my body
into hers from behind.
And as my hands moved
into places she did not expect,
and as my love began to rise
and make itself known,
she softly gasped just before she asked:
"What conditions would that be?"
Just then, I raised her sundress
to see she was not wearing anything beneath it;
so I quickly undid my belt
and bent her over the counter,
that by now, was almost as hard as me.
And as I slowly entered this amazing woman,
I whispered in her ear: "Conditions like these."

CLYDE HURLSTON

AFTER CAREFUL OBSERVATION

After careful observation,
I can see the side effects of love.
With so many buttons pushed,
it's a miracle there hasn't been a shove.
For it seems that my toxic trait,
is to miss you when you're gone.
While yours is wanting me to leave,
and being mad I'm not home.
I guess that's why you walk around,
projecting feelings of regret.
Eager to start arguing,
as if that's the only way to get you wet.
But baby you don't have to be a bad girl,
for you to be fucked like one.
Just arch your back for Daddy now,
and bite the sheets until I'm done.
Then I may forgive your past behavior,
as you're calling out for God.
And telling the sympathetic pillowcase,
how I am so very flawed.
And I'll continue hurting you,
with a love that gets so deep.
That you'll become a good girl for me again,
as I fuck you straight to sleep.

BENEATH THE VEIL

When it comes to you, my love,
I have often wondered
Just what hides beneath the veil.
What are the things you most desire,
Yet are the most reticent to request?
Has it been too long since I have tasted you?
Have you settled for gentle strokes
Instead of the sacred thrusts
That reached your very soul?
I know how much of your life
You are forced to control, darling.
Tell me, do you not crave
A safe place to surrender?
Or would you rather mount a love
That you could ride
Like the waves within your oceans?
All you have to do
Is come back to me, baby.
Your pleasure was all I ever cared about.
There is no need to hide yourself from me.
Veils have no place
Inside the castle we'll share.
If you want something from me,
All you have to do is ask, my love.

CLYDE HURLSTON

FOR THIS PEN MADE WONDERS (PART 1 OF 2)

I have written many times of longing;
but I'd like to think I've written just as much of love.
And it comes as no surprise to me,
that when I write of such things,
your name is never far behind.
It's as if I've loved you for so long,
that praising you has become a reflex.
But what I loved the most,
is that with this pen I could
overcome my modest means.
With this pen, I can write wonders.
With one stroke of this pen,
I could finally give you the world.
And with two strokes,
I could place the sun and moon
within your gentle hands;
knowing they each
paled in comparison to your smile.
Darling, I could gently write life into your lips,
and quickly write pain out of your heart.
I could selfishly write lust onto your tongue,
and eagerly write a welcome
for my monument between your legs.
I could lovingly write diamonds around your neck
and decidedly write diamonds on your fingers.
I could proudly write you
a castle upon the tallest hill
and successfully write you
a sports car in its garage.
But for some damn reason,
I can't seem to write you back to me.
In any form or fashion.
So I guess I'll have to keep writing,
until I can make my peace with that.

FOR THIS PEN MADE GODS
(PART 2 OF 2)

Although you would never say it aloud darling,
I know that you get a thrill
from seeing how many others wish
they could take your place inside these lines.
And I find it funny,
that despite not wanting to ever take your place
inside this imagined throne,
you still refuse to abdicate it to another.
Knowing good and goddamn well,
that my pen would've never learned your name,
had you not come crashing into my world
as yours began to crumble all those years ago.
So why is it that you seek so hard to find
your reflection in a mirror you've long since forsaken?
Because that behavior is the reason why
it's been so hard to forgive you for what you've done.
For here I thought we were two souls
experiencing a love worthy of the lore.
Now I see that you were only in it for one reason:
through works of art, muses tend to live forever.
And I did for you,
what he could never dream of doing:
I made you immortal.

CLYDE HURLSTON

WHEN TEMPTATION IS AN ART

For some, temptation was just a word.
For others, it became a skill.
Yet, she was the kind of a woman,
that turned temptation into an art form.
Every day she sought to rekindle a fire,
that other women had allowed to fall prey
to time and lack of fuel.
And how she did it was effortless.
Whether it was a suggestive phrase
or strategic photograph,
she had a myriad of ways.
The result was always the same:
a love that hardened like granite.
Eager and willing to be shared with her.
And luckily, her arrival was near.
It was as if the throbbing that I felt
was a countdown that I kept.
In anticipation of my repayment of this ache.
Which she would be made to feel,
one hard thrust at a time.
Until the once-referenced countdown was over,
and we were both ready to explode.
Because when temptation is an art,
the gods expect a mess to be made upon the canvas.
And so we made a masterpiece.

WHEN WORLDS COLLIDE

As we were in the midst of
another session of shared passion,
she asked me to read her
something from my new book.
The one you are now reading.
And while reading was the last thing
I intended to do upon this night,
I always aimed to please her.
And so, I began reciting
a piece I could easily remember.
But by the third thrust,
I realized she was no longer listening to me.
She was far too lost
in the symphony of sounds
made by our two worlds colliding.
And that's when I realized that poetry
can happen anywhere you make it.
But what made her a good girl,
was proving just how deep
she could fucking take it.

CLYDE HURLSTON

RECONSTRUCTION

She knew exactly what she wanted.
And she expected to get it,
without having to ask for it.
Because for her, misbehaving was only fun,
when it was followed by punishment.
So having looked deeply in her perfect eyes,
I realized she wanted to be destroyed.
One, hard thrust at a time.
Until she stopped saying my name,
because she couldn't remember her own.
But I also knew that when I was done with her,
she wanted to be held tightly.
So that she could come back together
within these large arms of mine.
For while there was a rush to be had in demolition,
love was found only in the reconstruction.

WORDS AS WATER

Darling, I hope you take
these words as water.
I hope when you look at them,
you see only the best of yourself
reflected back at you.
For I have written of you
more times than I can count.
Trying to convince the world
of things I already knew about you.
Eager to show them what your love
had made me feel capable of doing.
And even in moments
that I bore my pain after you left,
it was apparent to all who read,
just how much I loved you.
And I have to believe
that you know this was by design.
For although the circumstances
were far from ideal,
you are still the best thing
that has ever happened to me.
And now that there is a chance
that I can have your love again,
I will go through hell or high water
to feel every drop of it.

BATHE IN DARKNESS

I had spent forever waiting for you.
Even though you and I
Had danced in and out of
Each other's lives for years now.
I still waited.
Hoping and praying that eventually
You would come to your senses,
And realize where you belonged.
And it was here with me.
Because your impression
Still remains here, darling.
I can remember every detail
About those nights.
The same way I know
That you can still feel
The places I reached inside of you.
And you know damn well,
No one else fits as perfectly
Between my arms as you do.
You just have to remember your home.
Won't you come back
And bathe in this darkness with me, love?
Help me turn these black skies blue.
Give back to me
The one thing I never stopped loving:
And that, my dear, is you.

WITHIN YOUR WATERS

After all this time,
I thought you would see
That I was different.
I thought you could tell,
That while my lips do ache
For your love,
They would neve take
More than their fill.
For I only wished to see
Flowers grow within your waters.
Instead, I was left
Waiting upon dry land.
Having been weighed,
Measured,
Found wanting, and
Eventually dying of an unending thirst.
Whilst wishing I could be drowned,
In that which I had clearly lost.

CLYDE HURLSTON

NOT LETTING GO

She never would fucking listen...
She was as stubborn
As she was gorgeous.
I kept trying to tell her
That it was okay,
That she could let me go.
Because in the end,
This world would be
A much better place
Without me around.
I could just float away
Into the darkness
And not bother a single soul.
And I would drift
until I found another world
That was a better fit for someone
As out of place as me.
But she wouldn't hear of it.
She said if I needed space,
She'd buy me a fucking telescope instead.
But she wasn't letting me go anywhere.
She says I have too much left to do here.
She claims my pen
Is supposed to change the world.
And I just laughed.
How do you argue with someone
Whose love has already
Taken you to outer space and back?

CLAIMED IN DARKNESS

Despite all that I am clearly lacking,
I remain a blessed man.
For there are so many around the world,
that are suffering fates far worse than mine.
So many that would risk their lives
for the things I sometimes take for granted.
But having said that,
my greatest blessing is not a material object.
It is not the food, the clothing, or even the shelter
that I am fortunate enough to possess.
Friend, my greatest blessing is her.
The one that saved me from the hell within myself.
I can still remember it like it was yesterday;
though I still find it hard to believe.
With every single thing going on in her life,
somehow she saw me.
She would look at me and see the selflessness
with which I loved those around me.
She'd often be in awe, having read the sadness
and passions pouring out of my words.
And she would recoil in pain,
after witnessing the way I spoke about myself.
And it was clear she'd had enough.
So she decided to do something about it:
she would love me back to life.
After that first kiss, it was as if
she crawled into my eyes
and told the darkness she found there,
that it needed to leave, and fast.
"He belongs to me now," she said.
And so it was then that I was claimed in darkness.

CLYDE HURLSTON

THE WOMAN I LOVED

You have never known true love,
Unless you were given enough room
To be the truest version of yourself.
And that's exactly what she had with me.
True, the circumstances were far from ideal;
Still, my open arms were never her prison.
Because she was not
the type of woman you domesticated.
No, her wild was never tamed; only harnessed .
For she was not the obedient kind of woman,
Who would remain in the kitchen.
No, she was the kind of woman
That was far too busy
Breaking these generational curses.
She was the type of woman
That cared nothing for brand names,
As she was far more concerned
With making a name of her own.
And she was the kind of woman
That was submissive, only in the bedroom;
If and when she saw fit.
Yeah, in the past,
she would've been the kind of woman
That they would burn at the stake.
But here in the present, she became the fire.
So be sure to hide your forbidden fruits,
Because she is coming for what she is owed.
And that is why, she is the woman that I loved.

BELONG TO NO ONE

I would be lying,
If I said I was not in awe of her.
For I had never in my life seen
Fearlessness look as good
As it did on her.
Each time she spoke,
The hair on my arm would stand up.
Because she spoke without malice;
And yet, her every sentence was formed
With razor-sharp intent.
She never once minced her words;
All she did was shatter expectations.
And so it wasn't strange for me
To stare at her in disbelief.
It was rare for someone like me
To be at a loss for words.
But I found that the reverence in my silence
Was the only thing that did her justice.
For I had never seen a woman
Without a weapon
So ready to wage war.
And I had never seen a woman
Without a partner
Abstain from love
As if it brought death.
She would belong to no one.
Not even to nature itself.

CLYDE HURLSTON

SHE WILL BE HEARD

It has long been said
That hellfire pales in comparison
To a woman scorned.
And I know this to be true.
For I have seen,
Thankfully only from afar,
When the fire in her eyes
Caused tears to evaporate into smoke.
That is when the Earth itself
Will think twice before turning.
And I envy not the poor soul
Who had provoked such a state in her.
Because they have knowingly
Or unknowingly unleashed
Centuries of pent up rage and frustration.
For every supposed witch
That was burned at the stake.
And for every woman
That stood her ground
And was then maligned by
The history books of men,
She will have her day.
Despite the intentions of
Wrinkled, judgmental hands
Of the past and present
Reaching slowly toward her mouth,
She will not be silenced any longer.
She has been quiet for far too long.
No matter what happens
From this day forth,
She will be heard.

SHE SPOKE LIFE

I never understood how she did it.
To me, it was as if she had
some kind of magical powers.
How else could you explain
what she did so effortlessly?
After earning her trust,
she told me of the myriad
of horrors that she had been through.
And I wondered how life could force
someone to endure so much.
Still, I never once heard her complain
about her circumstances.
She had a faith that was as strong
as it was quiet.
For she never once forced
her beliefs onto others.
She simply embodied them.
It seemed like she could take
the darkness of this world
and turn it into light.
I'm certain this ability
had to weigh on her at times.
Still, she never spoke ill of anyone.
Instead, she spoke life
into everyone that she loved.
And for that,
she will always be my hero.

CLYDE HURLSTON

THE EPITAPH OF A FOOL

Yes, dear reader… I am a man.
And for the longest time,
it was my absolute honor
to venerate the woman.
I did this so much,
it became second nature to me.
Growing up in a family full of strong women,
I was surrounded by the sacred feminine
with each step I took.
Respect, empathy, and consideration
would become my calling cards.
And as I grew older and began to seek
a woman for my own,
each prospective lover felt like a divine gift.
Without realizing it, I began placing them
upon pedestals in my mind.
With each becoming more uncomfortable
with such reverence by the minute.
And soon, without fail,
my predictable behavior led to rejection.
All because I mistakenly believed myself
to be unworthy of them.
Unaware that these thoughts
would become a self-fulfilling prophecy.
For a woman's innate intuition
could sense such a thing,
and was seemingly repulsed by it.
But now that I am older,
I have learned to maintain the balance
I have so sorely lacked in my youth.
No longer do I believe myself unworthy.
Quite the contrary.
I look around and I believe

THE SACRED GIFT OF FIRE

there will be one woman that deserves me.
Still, I can't help but gaze at the women I see
and still feel those familiar feelings of awe.
Since I know their power all too well.
Yet, having said that, if this train of thought
is to make me a fool,
let that be my epitaph then.
For I would much rather be a supposed fool
for choosing to respect a woman,
than to ever be the kind of monster
that intentionally and consciously harmed one.

CLYDE HURLSTON

SHE SEDUCED THE SUN

Though my ways are changing,
when I think of her,
I find myself falling back into old habits.
At the end of the day,
I know she is only human;
one with a myriad of moods and imperfections.
But that still doesn't stop me
from being in awe of her.
Sometimes I look at her and
I think of what a privilege it is to be alive.
So that I may bear witness to such splendor.
So that I may use my gift
to document her as Grace made flesh.
Truth be told dear friends,
it is because of her,
that I used to envy the sunlight.
Why? You may ask.
And the answer is simple, really.
Because sunlight gets to touch her skin everyday,
and I do not.
Such a blessing was not bestowed to me.
But the more I think about it,
I have come to believe
that she has seduced the sun.
How else can she glow the way she does?
My God, it's as if the sun rises in the morning
just to get the first look at her.
And I imagine that the night waits
as long as possible before overtaking the day,
just to get a glimpse
of her silhouette upon the ground.
So now that I've said that,
try and imagine what seeing her shape

beneath the sun does to me.
Fuck, if she only knew what it does...
It makes me want to taste the eternal summer
she hides within herself.
Just one smile from her and
I want to drink sunlight off of her in places
I should not talk about in public.
But since I am not allowed inside of her,
I must instead get these words out of me.
So let the record show that she exists.
She was not a tall tale or a creative myth;
nor was she a product of my lonely imagination.
No, my friends, she was simply the one
that caused my imagination to run wild.
To run wild beneath the sun.
Always finding its way back to her.

CLYDE HURLSTON

THESE GRATEFUL HANDS

Very few things
awaken a soul as starved as this,
more than a prolonged entrance
into the temple.
Having been left outside
in the elements for so long,
It is truly a transcendent feeling
for this weary traveler
to be welcomed this way.
So warmly, so deeply.
As if this chamber were made
for eye and I alone.
By the gods, it is almost as if
one would have to fight with everything they have,
just to hold themselves together in here.
For upon mere arrival in this sacred temple,
it is quite difficult not to have
an out-of-body experience.
But through great effort,
I am able to maintain my vigor.
All the while, knowing places like this
can only be visited by the worthy.
Here in the holiest of spaces,
room is only made for those
with unquestioning hearts
and the firmest of beliefs.
And in my heart, I believe that is why
I was graced with the ability
to make myself at home within these walls.
Seeing as I have always treated each visit
with the reverence it deserved.
For these grateful hands
have never knocked upon the temple doors.
They have simply come together in prayer,
for the chance to hold them open.

MORE HUMAN THAN ANGEL

Darling, since your departure,
I have wondered a great many things.
But the thought I come back to most often is:
what did you ever see in me to begin with?
Sure, people will claim
that is not the outside that matters,
it's what is on the inside that counts.
But if I had a dollar for every time
I've heard such things,
then I could surely buy a new exterior.
Yet, that truly never mattered to you.
At least, I don't think it did.
Because I still remember the way you looked at me.
It was a mixture of love, lust, and admiration.
And after every single time you kissed me,
I would wonder what I ever did
to be the object of such a gaze.
And while time has proven you
to be more human than angel;
if you didn't wear a halo in those moments,
then you damn sure deserved one.
Because you gave hope to a beast
that believed it deserved none.
And for doing that,
I will forever keep a place in my heart for you.

CLYDE HURLSTON

UNTIL ARMS FELT LIKE WINGS

Darling, if my words do nothing else,
I pray they remind you exactly who you are.
Because I once told you
that I believed the sun rose every morning,
just to see your face.
And I never believed in angels,
until I witnessed your loving grace.
And yes, I know the past few years have been rough.
But you must remember a few things:
For one, strength has known your name,
long before it ever blessed my tongue.
Two, I've seen the compassion in your touch,
make coal feel as if it were diamonds.
And three, courage has lived inside of you,
long before you ever made my heart feel at home.
So tell me, love, how could I not tell this world of you?
I will tell them all how you stretched out your arms,
until they felt like wings.
Knowing that you no longer
had to worry about falling.
Because you have a man
that has been waiting his whole life to catch you.

A REMINDER FOR THE MOON

I know you're struggling right now.
I can tell from the weight of your silence,
that you feel like breaking down.
But deep down, we both know
that you will do no such thing.
Why, you ask?
Because you're a warrior.
I don't think you even know
the meaning of the word defeat.
Or submit.
Just remember that this too shall pass.
You have a whole life in front of you
that is just dying to be lived.
The days and nights are lining up,
just waiting for you.
And sure, it hurts now.
Darling, the darkness never feels good.
Just remember that the darkness
will teach you of yourself.
And it will teach you how to appreciate the stars.
Because it's then that they're easiest to see.
But never forget: the darkness cannot hurt you.
And would you like to know why?
It's because you are the goddamn moon.
That is when you shine the best.

CLYDE HURLSTON

PATI HODIE, ORTUM CRAS

Oh, my child, I know it hurts...
but you must endure.
For this life is but a lesson.
One that must be learned
through struggle and strife.
If nothing moves, nothing changes.
And without shedding blood or tears,
a soul never grows.
So you must continue!
You must suffer today,
so that you may rise and reign tomorrow.
And while the story of your body
may end with bones,
you must come to see
that the story of your soul
always ends on thrones.
That is why I once again bid you to endure!
For you are made of stars;
and the word quit
was never written amongst them.

BY ANY OTHER NAME

Most will never know the pain
of being an esoteric lover in a truly profane world.
For I used to believe that the woman
was the most sacred thing an imperfect man
like me could ever hope to touch.
And for that belief
I was often painted as a fool or simp,
by the blade and chalice alike.
Yet, if I was lucky enough
to survive the pitfalls of that perception,
it was then that I was made to be a martyr.
Dying on metaphoric crosses
for the sins of other men
that were far lesser than I.
As if Pilate himself had thrown his thumb
in the downward direction and sealed my fate.
I could not fathom the truths
shaped like spears in my side:
That which I sought most in life would run from me,
simply because of the reverence I had for it.
And those who never held it
in any sort of regard,
would receive it in abundance.
Such a fate would be Hell by any other name!
For what would you call a state
where you could only dream of Heaven?
Never being allowed to enter
the Garden of a Goddess;
nor reaching the holiest parts of her Temple.
Friend, I would call it Hell;
the only place I have ever known as home.

CLYDE HURLSTON

THE STORY REMAINS THE SAME

Darling, those that have been paying attention,
surely know the story by now.
For they have visited these pages
and read all about how I yearned for you.
And how brightly I burned for you.
They know that with just a look from you,
I could produce smoke.
And they recall how just one kiss from you,
could raise a monument as hard as granite.
But what they need to know now,
is how you feel.
And why you keep running from a love
that could not only fill libraries one by one,
but also made you lose count
of the number of times you would cum.

LET THERE BE NO DOUBT

Darling, when all the dust has settled,
when all the smoke has cleared,
and after your careful hands
have turned my final page...
Let there be no doubt of my existence!
For between these lines
I have answered questions,
many lacked the courage to ask themselves.
Between these lines,
I have loved and I have lost.
I have made love
and I've fucked with reckless abandon.
I have built pedestals and I have spat rage.
All of it from my own heart.
All of it from my own soul.
All of it from my own pen.
Poured directly onto this page,
And poured directly into your own mind.
And I say now,
With every ounce of conviction.
Every drop of hubris.
And missing every trace of humility...
I say now, before the gods
And my fellow men as witness.
Let there be no fucking doubt,
That you loved every minute of it.

CLYDE HURLSTON

END OF ACT 3

"I make love with a focus and intensity that most people reserve for sleep" - Dark Jar Tin Zoo

"When sex involves all the senses intensely, it can be like a mystical experience." - Jim Morrison

"This last night we tear into each other, as if to wound, as if to find the key to everything before morning." - Michael Ondaatje

CLYDE HURLSTON

"We are all born sexual creatures, thank
God, but it's a pity so many people despise
and crush this natural gift."
- Marilyn Monroe

"Sex is always about emotions. Good sex
is about free emotions; bad sex is about
blocked emotions."
- Deepak Chopra

"Love without sex is still the most efficient
form of hell known to man."
- Peter Porter

"There is no religion but sex and music."
- Sting

THE SACRED GIFT OF FIRE

"The Sacred Gift Of Fire" Art by Bowie

"The way you slam your body into mine reminds me I'm alive."
- Richard Silken

CLYDE HURLSTON

Reflections Of Janus recommends these other books from Clyde R. Hurlston